An Essay on the Need to Revise Marx' and Engels' Historical Materialism

Ib Gram-Jensen
An Essay on the Need to Revise Marx' and Engels' Historical Materialism

© 2025 Ib Gram-Jensen
Publisher: BoD · Books on Demand, Strandvejen 100,
2900 Hellerup, bod@bod.dk
Print: Libri Plureos GmbH, Friedensallee 273, 22763 Hamborg, Tyskland
ISBN: 978-87-7145-857-2

For Susanne

Contents

Introduction.

Marx' and Engels' historical materialism suffers from serious weaknesses, some of which have been dealt with in a number of texts by this writer. Firstly, their conception of the dialectic of forces and relations of production as the motive power of historical development and transformations does not seem tenable. Secondly, their idea that the transition from capitalism to socialism and eventually classless communist society is inevitable, which is connected with that conception, does not seem tenable either. And thirdly, the question whether, and if so how, a workable classless society can actually be established and maintained remains open – and is left open by this essay as well, as it is beyond the competence of this writer to give any definite answer.

The title of my previous book on these questions, *A Revised Historical Materialism*, of the first essay of which the present text can in many ways be considered an extended and revised version, was chosen rather than something like the subtitle of Meiksins Wood's *Democracy Against Capitalism*, namely *Renewing Historical Materialism*, as what is argued is not only the need to *add* something new to Marx' and Engels' historical materialism, but also the need to *cut something away* from it: their conception of the dialectic of forces and relations of production as the motive power of historical development and transformations, and their belief that historical development and transformations are ruled by laws comparable to those ruling natural development, before substituting something new for the excised elements – which are, moreover, some of its very central ones.

What is very explicitly stated in *A Revised Historical Materialism* is that the revision is *not* a matter of rejecting the revolutionary transition from capitalism to socialism and eventually classless communist society, or any idea of accomplishing it by means of gradual reforms: both reformist and gradualist strategies are rejected, and the grounds for rejecting them are stated.[1] Moreover, a premise for the whole discussion is the belief that an effectively classless society can *only* be based on the *effectively collective* command of the means, process and outcome of production. Which, in its turn, requires a genuinely democratic society as the precondition for effectively *collective* decisions on public affairs, with all the freedoms required for the establishment and functioning of "an association in which the free development of each is the condition for the free development of all."[2]

The two crucial elements in the intellectual heritage left by Marx and Engels are the critique of political economy and their historical materialism. The critique of political economy identifies the appropriation of surplus value and surplus labour by means of "the equal exchange between free agents which reproduces, hourly and daily, inequality and oppression"[3] in capitalist production. What this critique of political economy, and of the capitalist mode of production and type of society, cannot, in itself, offer is a strategy for the substitution of this exploitative mode by a classless, that is, communist, society or even an answer to the question whether this is possible or not.

Therefore a theory, or at least hypothesis, about the nature of the process of historical development and transformations from one type of society, defined by a dominant mode of production, to another is relevant – and according to Marx

---

[1] Gram-Jensen, *A Revised Historical Materialism*, p. 114-116.
[2] Marx & Engels, *Manifest der Kommunistischen Partei*, p. 482. Cf. Gram-Jensen, *A Revised Historical Materialism*, p. 113.
[3] Anderson, *Lineages of the Absolutist State*, p. 403.

and Engels, the historical materialism they sketched as a hypothesis about this process lead to the conclusion that the transition from capitalism to socialism and eventually classless communist society would inevitably be accomplished through the agency of the proletariat, the class created and exploited by capitalism. Hence the importance of the *laws* assumed to rule the process of historical development and transformations, and of the conception of the dialectic of forces and relations of production assumed to be its motive power.

Thus, the two elements which are irreducible to each other: the critique of political economy, the analysis of capitalism and capitalist exploitation, on the one hand, and historical materialism, the hypothesis about the nature and terminal of historical development and transformations in what Marx designated "the prehistory of human society",[4] on the other. The latter is unmistakably – and explicitly – imbued with a Hegelian dialectic turned upside down, and thus changed from an idealistic into a materialistic dialectic, in order to find its rational kernel.[5] And according to it, historical development is "a process of natural history ruled by laws that are not only independent of the will, consciousness and intentions of people, but on the contrary determine their will, consciousness and intentions."[6] Hence Marx' and Engels' historical materialism is marked by a fundamental *tension* in terms of the relationship between historical determinism on the one hand and human agency on the other.

In the present context, the point is not whether Marx and Engels' interpretation of Hegel is more or less correct, but

---

[4] Marx, *A Contribution to the Critique of Political Economy*, p. 22 (*MEW*, 13, p. 9).
[5] Marx, *Das Kapital*, 1, p. 27.
[6] Marx, *Das Kapital*, 1, p. 26.

what their "inverted" dialectic of historical development and transformations is and implies. And this is summarised in Marx' 1859 Preface to *A Contribution to the Critique of Political Economy* and suggested by various other passages in his and Engels' finished texts, notably the *Manifesto, Capital* and *Anti-Dühring*, but also, sketchily, adumbrated in *Die deutsche Ideologie* and discussed or alluded to in various other texts, e. g. the *Grundrisse*, and letters of theirs.

Thus, the emphasis is on demonstrating from the textual evidence that the abovementioned determinism *is* indeed found in Marx' and Engels' historical materialism, and on the reasons *why* it must be considered untenable as well as rendering their historical materialism inconsistent: there is an ineradicable tension in it between the notion of human agents as the makers of their own history (on given conditions) on the one hand and their notion of historical development and transformations as a quasi-natural process ruled by laws comparable to those of natural development, based on their conception of the dialectic of forces and relations of production as the motive power of historical development and transformations, on the other. Some additional questions are, however, dealt with too, mostly in order to give a more precise impression of the nature of the recommended revision, which includes demarcating it from some other suggested alternatives to Marx' and Engels' historical materialism.

The required revision may, then, be summarised as follows:

1. The conception of the dialectic of forces and relations of production has to be substituted by that of the interaction between social circumstances and agency as the motive power of historical developments and transformations.
2. Engels' idea of conflicting human wills cancelling out, thus producing parallelograms of power giving

rise to historical development which thus proceeds in the manner of a natural process and is essentially subject to the same laws of motion,[7] must be abandoned along with that of history being ruled by laws comparable to those ruling natural development, determining the will, consciousness and intentions of agents.[8]

3. Human beings must be *consistently* acknowledged as the makers of their own history under the given and inherited circumstances with which they are directly confronted, and the theoretical and strategic implications of this acknowledgment must be accepted.[9]

Finally, it may be added that (structural) determination must be understood in the Wrightean sense of the delimitation of a field of the possible, with pressures and probabilities, within which actual historical outcomes eventuate.[10] And that the question of class capacities[11] is important when these outcomes are to be accounted for.

---

[7] Engels, "Engels an Joseph Bloch in Königsberg, 21./22. September 1890", p. 464.

[8] Marx, *Das Kapital*, 1, p. 25-27.

[9] Marx, *The Eighteenth Brumaire of Louis Bonaparte*, p. 146 (*MEW*, 8, p. 115).

[10] Wright, *Class, Crisis and the State*, p. 15-17.

[11] Levine & Wrigth, passim. Wrigth, Levine & Sober, Part I.

1. The Evidence.

The argument for this revision of Marx' and Engels' historical materialism also involves a critique of interpretations of it to the effect that there is *no* determinist element in it, which thus gloss over the gap left in it by the lack of a *strategy* for the transition from capitalism to socialism and eventually class-less communist society once its determinist assumptions are abandoned. This critique is therefore partly motivated by this strategic consideration, partly by the sheer, and rather surprising, defectiveness of several interpreters' readings of Marx and Engels.[12]

The primary, first-hand evidence of Marx' and Engels' thoughts – and the only primary, first-hand evidence – is their texts, among which those "Books and major essays that were published under the control of the writer, with the usual opportunity for correction, revision, etc." must be considered the most reliable.[13] At full length, Draper's list of different categories of texts runs as follows, in descending order of reliability:

> 1. Books and major essays that were published under the control of the writer, with the usual opportunity for correction, revision, etc. (Most of Marx's or Engels' major works will come to mind as examples.)
> 2. Articles published under the control of the writer.
> a. Articles composed as political statements, for a political audience, and signed; in short, intended for the purpose they are used for.

---

[12] Cf. Gram-Jensen, the second essay in *Experience and Historical Materialism, Structure, Theory and Agency*, Part One, ch.s 2-3 and Appendix Three, the first, second and seventh essays in *A Critique of Mau: Mute Compulsion and Other Essays* and the first and second essays in *A Revised Historical Materialism*.

[13] Draper, *Karl Marx's Theory of Revolution*, II, p. 3.

b. Articles in which remarks on issues occur only in passing, often elliptically.

c. Journalistic articles, written as hack work, perhaps not even signed.

3. Articles published not under the control of the writer. Perhaps the most extreme case is that of *New York Tribune* articles that were rewritten or added to at will by the editors.

4. Unpublished manuscripts.

a. Unfinished or fragmentary, often never reviewed or revised – unfinished for various possible reasons, including dissatisfaction with the work.

b. Finished – but unpublished for various possible reasons, including dissatisfaction.

5. Letters. The circumstances of a letter, including its addressee, must always be taken into account. When writing to Engels, Marx takes much for granted and does not have to phrase his thoughts as they come to the pen in order to avoid ignorant or malicious misinterpretation. Some letters to others are diplomatizing. All letters are timebound: opinions expressed (for example, about people) may change. Letters are prime examples of ad-hoc writings that cannot be usefully quoted until the context is evaluated.

a. Circular letters. These are very like political statements, more like considered articles than casual correspondence.

b. "Educational" letters. Written to strangers in some cases, to party leaders in others, these are written with some conscious effort to set down a view; but even so, without the responsibilities entailed by publication.

c. Intimate letters, where all is "thinking aloud" and no effort is made to avoid possible misunderstandings by a third party. Most of the correspondence between Marx and Engels comes under this head. Very often, general-sounding statements have specific contexts and meanings.

d. Casual or ad-hoc letters, perhaps hastily dashed off, given little or no consideration of any kind.

6. Private notes, notebooks, and workbooks. These were not only not written for publication but were often written in a personal "shorthand" or in a telegraphic and allusive style, intended only for the writer's eyes. The aforementioned *Grundrisse* is an example of a long work in this style; Marx's "Conspectus of Bakunin's Book &c." is a shorter and more fragmentary case.[14]

Again, in what I have written on this, the focus is not on the extent to which, and how, Marx' and Engels' conception of the nature (and laws) of the process of historical development is inspired by Hegel or anyone else, but on what this conception *is*. And, therefore, on how Marx and Engels themselves present it in their texts.

We cannot ignore or dismiss explicit statements in these texts which are recurrent and demonstrably form integral parts of the theoretical framework presented in the texts unless there are very strong, and well-authenticated, reasons for doing so. And if we want to establish what Marx and Engels thought and wanted to communicate – including changes in this over time – it seems logical to attach greater weight to what they published, or wanted to publish but were prevented from publishing by external circumstances, than to what they left unpublished. In other words, we should not, for example, make it a rule to interpret concepts and arguments in *Capital* to make them fit those in the *Grundrisse*, let alone reject them

---

[14] Draper, *Karl Marx's Theory of Revolution*, II, *The Politics of Social Classes*, p. 3-4. As argued in *Experience and Historical Materialism*, section d. of the second essay, Draper himself misreads the *Manifesto*.

or try to explain them away if they cannot be read with the *Grundrisse* as a key to "what Marx really meant" by what he wrote in *Capital*. Nor, of course, should we interpret and screen Marx' and Engels' concepts and argumentation according to what we think they *should* have meant – that is, "represent modifications and additions to Marx's thought as 'interpretations' or 'readings' of Marx's texts."[15]

What we should do is to read Marx' and Engels' texts loyally, that is, to do our best to establish as precisely as possible what Marx and Engels intended to communicate, and then state and argue our own position on this as clearly and cogently as possible. While the conceptual apparatus they inherited from others should certainly be recognised, the temptation to "decode" their texts by reading them in a "Hegelian" or "Spinozist", "Darwinian" or whatever other sense, no matter what the sentences in the texts seem to mean when read straightforwardly, should be resisted. Even when Marx and Engels state that they are influenced by Hegel or others, as they do in various places, the *way* in which they read and followed them must be deciphered from their own reasoning.

Marx' and Engels' predictions of the inevitable transition from capitalism to socialism and eventually classless communist society are explicit and recur in central texts of theirs, including ones published under their control, from the mid-1840s and on, and based on their conception of the dialectic of forces and relations of production as the motive power of historical development and transformations which likewise recurs in these texts from the mid-1840s and on, and forms an integral part of their historical materialism as presented more or less systematically in the texts, e. g. *Die deutsche Ideologie*, *The Poverty of Philosophy*, the *Manifesto of the Communist*

---

[15] Timpanaro, p. 194.

Party, the Preface to *A Contribution to the Critique of Political Economy*, *Capital* and *Anti-Dühring.*

These recurrent predictions and the arguments on which they are based cannot be dismissed as mere exhortatory cheering on the troops without demonstration by means of very strong evidence that Marx and Engels themselves did not believe in them – evidence which, to the best knowledge of this writer, nobody has so far presented: the words opening the first section of the *Manifesto*,[16] which have been referred to by various writers,[17] do not amount to such evidence.

It is also evident from the texts that Marx and Engels based their expectations and predictions precisely on their conception of the dialectic of forces and relations of production as the motive power of historical development and transformations.

[16] Marx & Engels, *Manifest der Kommunistischen Partei*, p. 462.
[17] Draper, *The Adventures of the Communist Manifesto*, p. 210, p. 243. Gasper. Sørensen, "Den historiske materialisme i lyset af nyere diskussion om social handlen og social objektivitet", p. 26-27. Collier, p. 143-144. Thing, p. 82-83.

2. Marx' and Engels' Historical Materialism.

In section ix of his essay "The Poverty of History", Thompson called attention to the distinction between structural and historical analysis with their different heuristics as a problem in historical materialism left unresolved by Marx and Engels. And to their "historicist notions of lawed and pre-determined development"[18] which are part of this problematic. A problematic also involving the problem of how to understand the meaning and significance of the interconnected concepts of "relative autonomy" and "determination in the last instance".[19]

Marx' and Engels' historical materialism is a theory or hypothesis about the nature of the process of historical development and transformations (that is, the transitions from one type of society (defined by a specific dominant mode of production) to another), with the conception of the dialectic of forces and relations of production as the motive power of this process as its core element. This conception is the major problem with their historical materialism, while some unsuccessful attempts to reconcile it and its implications with the conception of human beings as the makers of their own history, which are dealt with below, are less crucial, but symptomatic of the tension in their historical materialism between these two conceptions and their respective implications. The conception of the dialectic of forces and relations as the motive power of historical development and transformations is found in their texts from the mid-1840s and on, with its classical formulation in Marx' 1859 Preface to *A Contribution to the Critique of Political Economy*.

---

[18] Thompson, *The Poverty of Theory and Other Essays*, p. 69.
[19] Thompson, *The Poverty of Theory and Other Essays*, p. 67-68.

[.....]. At a certain stage of development, the material productive forces of society come into conflict with the existing relations of production or – this merely expresses the same thing in legal terms – with the property relations within the framework of which they have operated hitherto. From forms of development of the productive forces these relations turn into their fetters. Then begins an era of social revolution. The changes in the economic foundation lead sooner or later to the transformation of the whole immense superstructure. In studying such transformations it is always necessary to distinguish between the material transformation of the economic conditions of production, which can be determined with the precision of natural science, and the legal, political, religious, artistic or philosophic – in short, ideological forms in which men become conscious of this conflict and fight it out. Just as one does not judge an individual by what he thinks about himself, so one cannot judge such a period of transformation by its consciousness, but, on the contrary, this consciousness must be explained from the contradictions of material life, from the conflict existing between the social forces of production and the relations of production. No social order is ever destroyed before all the productive forces for which it is sufficient have been developed, and new superior relations of production never replace older ones before the material conditions for their existence have matured within the framework of the old society. Mankind thus inevitably sets itself only such tasks as it is able to solve, since closer examination will always show that the problem itself arises only when the material conditions for its solution are already present or at least in the course of formation. In broad outline, the Asiatic, ancient, feudal and modern bourgeois modes of production may be designated as epochs marking progress in the economic development of society. The bourgeois mode of production is the last antagonistic form of the social process of production – antagonistic not in the sense of individual antagonism but of an antagonism that emanates from the individuals' social conditions of existence – but the productive forces developing within bourgeois society create also the material conditions for a solution of this antagonism. The prehistory of human society accordingly closes with this social formation.[20]

This conception is the core element in Marx' and Engels' historical materialism because it serves as the very explanation why such transitions take place, and must take place: when the further development of the productive forces is fettered by the relations of production. Marx' *magnum opus, Capital,* is likewise informed by this conception on which his prediction of the inevitable transition from capitalism to socialism and eventually classless communist society, the leap of humanity, brought about by the victory of the proletariat and the fall of the bourgeoisie, from the realm of necessity to the realm of freedom terminating the prehistory of human society, is based: what are the words in *Capital,* 1, ch. 24.7 on the historical tendency of capitalist accumulation that the working class is "a class always increasing in numbers, and disciplined, united, organized by the very mechanism of capitalist production itself",[21] or those in the *Manifesto* that, "The advance of industry, whose involuntary promoter is the bourgeoisie, replaces the isolation of the labourers, due to competition, by their revolutionary combination, due to association",[22] or those in Marx' letter to Annenkow that, "With the acquisition

---

[20] Marx, *A Contribution to the Critique of Political Economy,* p. 20-22 (*MEW,* 13, p. 8-9).
[21] Marx, *Das Kapital,* 1, p. 790-791 (translation in Engels, *Anti-Dühring,* p. 160).
[22] Marx & Engels, *Manifest der Kommunistischen Partei,* p. 474.

of new forces of production, people change their mode of production",[23] if not so many promises that the isolation of class struggle[24] will be broken by the very development of capitalist productive forces and capitalist society itself? That is, more precisely, by the dialectic of forces and relations of production?

Marx' and Engels' expectations and predictions are if not based on, then related to the structural analysis of capitalism from which the conflict between the (fundamental) interests of the capitalist class (the bourgeoisie) and those of the working class (the proletariat) exploited by the capitalists is deduced. Their conception of the dialectic of forces and relations of production as the motive power of historical development and transformations is coupled with their expectation that the proletariat will be "increasing in numbers, and disciplined, united, organized by the very mechanism of the process of capitalist production itself."[25] These two elements in their historical materialism confirm each other, the latter rendering the expectation and prediction which is part of the other, more general one, more credible – there is not just a general law of historical development and transformations according to which capitalism is bound to be substituted by socialism and eventually classless communist society, the growing class capacity of the proletariat, the gravediggers of the bourgeoisie produced by the bourgeoisie itself is derivable from the structural analysis of capital(ism), and observable from the actual development of capitalist society.

---

[23] Marx, "Brief an P. W. Annenkow vom 28. Dezember 1846", p. 549.
[24] The limitation of social practice (i. e. agents' responses to their "lived" reality) to such forms as do not objectively threaten to disrupt the type of society and the dominant relations of production (Gram-Jensen, *Structure, Agency and Theory*, p. 1329).
[25] Marx, *Das Kapital*, 1, p. 790-791. Engels, *Anti-Dühring*, p. 160 (*MEW*, 20, p. 124).

The very conception of the fettering of the development of the forces of production by the relations of production is, or seems to be, somewhat ambiguous. In *Die deutsche Ideologie*, Marx and Engels stated that,

> We have shown that at the present time individuals *must* abolish private property, because the productive forces and forms of intercourse have developed so far that, under the domination of private property, they have become destructive forces, and because the contradiction between the classes has reached its extreme limits. Finally, we have shown that the abolition of private property and of the division of labour is itself the union of individuals on the basis created by modern productive forces and world intercourse.[26]

Here, the emphasis is not on the development of the productive forces being hampered by the relations of production, but on the negative consequences of the capitalist integument of this development, the turning of the potential technological development into negative effects on the lives of agents which is also the theme of Marx' speech "Rede auf der Jahresfeier des "People's paper" am 14. April 1856 in London".

---

[26] Marx & Engels, *Die deutsche Ideologie*, p. 424 (translation from Marx & Engels, *The German Ideology*, Lawrence & Wishart, London 1965, Progress Publishers, Moscow 1968, p. 495. As Marx remarked in his 1846 letter to Annenkow, he is using the word "intercourse" (French: commerce) in its widest German sense (Marx, "Marx an Pawel Wassiljewitsch Annenkow in Paris, 28. Dezember [1846]", p. 549), that is, covering more or less all kinds of relations, exchange and interaction between people, thus also covering relations of production (cf. Marx & Engels, *Manifest der Kommunistischen Partei*, p. 464: "Wir sehen also, wie die moderne Bourgeoisie selbst das Produkt eines langen Entwicklungsganges, einer Reihe von Umwälzungen in der Produktions- und Verkehrsweise ist").

In the *Manifesto*, as well as in ch. 24.7 of *Capital* on the historical tendency of capitalist accumulation, the abovementioned hampering or blocking of the development of the productive forces is emphasised:

> We see then: the means of production and of exchange, on whose foundation the bourgeoisie built itself up, were generated in feudal society. At a certain stage in the development of these means of production and of exchange, the conditions under which feudal society produced and exchanged, the feudal organization of agriculture and manufacturing industry, in one word, the feudal relations of property became no longer compatible with the already developed productive forces; they became so many fetters. They had to be burst asunder; they were burst asunder.[27]

But after all too much should not be made of the different more or less subtle differences of meaning which may be detected in the various relevant passages written in various contexts at different times. What is unmistakable is the fundamental idea of the dialectic of forces and relations of production as the motive power of historical development and transformations in the course of the prehistory of human society, the era of class societies, eras of social revolution occurring when the relations of production become fetters on the development of the material productive forces, and with the class with an interest in the transition to a new social order and the further development of the productive forces as the revolutionary agent of transition. And the success of this revolutionary class is, according to Marx and Engels, guaranteed by two things: firstly, the very question of the transition to a new social order will not arise before all the productive forces for which the existing social order is sufficient have been

---

[27] Marx & Engels, *Manifest der Kommunistischen Partei*, p. 467.

developed, *and* the material conditions for the new order have matured within the framework of the old one (the latter being true by definition), and secondly, because the potentially revolutionary class will be *forced* to accomplish the transformation, and, in the case of the working class in capitalist society, because capitalist development itself furthers the development of the class capacities the workers need in order to accomplish it.[28]

How, then, is this dialectic, *as an actual causality in history*, to be accounted for? In a teleological context, the answer is obvious, but hardly supportable in terms of human agency, if this agency is not reducible to a mere bearer or support of teleological causation – a reduction explicitly rejected by Marx and Engels in the mid-1840s.[29]

If such teleological causation or determination of human agency is *not* assumed, what is the basis for considering the dialectic of forces and relations of production as a law of historical development determining the will, consciousness and intentions of human agents, as a Russian reviewer did, his words to this effect being approvingly quoted by Marx in the Afterword to the second edition of *Capital*?

> For Marx only one thing is important: to find the law of the phenomena the investigation of which he is engaged in. And not only the law ruling them insofar as they have a finished form and constitute a whole [*in einem Zusammenhang stehn*], as it is observed in a given period, is important to him. Most important of all to him is the law of their transformation, their develop-

---

[28] Cf. Marx & Engels, *Manifest der Kommunistischen Partei*, p. 467-474. Marx, *Das Kapital*, 1, ch. 24.7. Engels, *Anti-Dühring*, p. 188-189, p. 332 (*MEW*, 20, p. 146-147, p. 261 ff).
[29] Marx & Engels, *Die heilige Familie*, p. 98; *Die deutsche Ideologie*, p. 45.

ment, i.e. the transition from one form to another, from one order of the whole to another. [.....] it is quite sufficient when, along with the necessity of the present order, he demonstrates at the same time the necessity of a different order into which the former must inevitably pass, quite regardless of people believing it or not, of their being conscious or unconscious of this. Marx considers the social movement a process of natural history ruled by laws that are not only independent of the will, consciousness and intentions of people, but on the contrary determine [*bestimmen*] their will, consciousness and intentions. [.....] The scientific value of such investigation lies in the explanation [*Aufklärung*] of the specific laws ruling the origin, existence, development, death of a given social organism and its substitution by another, higher one. And the book by Marx actually has this value.

Marx' comment was: "Depicting what he calls my real method so accurately [*treffend*] and, as far as my personal application of it is concerned, so favourably, what has the author depicted but the dialectical method?"[30]

Neither Marx nor Engels offer any definitive answer, but at best this confidence in the dialectic of forces and relations of

---

[30] Marx, *Das Kapital*, 1, p. 25-27. The reviewer's words about Marx' opinion that historical development and transformations are a process ruled by (quasi-)natural laws are confirmed by Marx' remarks about the "natural laws" arising from capitalist production and working with "iron-hard necessity" (Marx, *Das Kapital*, 1, p. 12), his emphasis on the "natural law" of social development and "natural (*naturgemäße*) phases of development (ibid., p. 15-16), and his statement that he considers "the development of the economic social formation a process of natural history" (ibid., p. 16) in the Preface to the 1st edition of *Capital*. Cf. Marx, "Brief an die Redaktion der "Otetschestwennyje Sapiski"" (November 1877 (?)), p. 108-111).

production as the motive power of historical development and transformations can be considered a *hypothesis*, expressed by Marx and Engels as the confidence that agents, more precisely the potentially revolutionary class, that is, the class with an interest in the continued development of the productive forces, will respond to the fettering of the development of the productive forces by the relations of production by effecting a historical transformation, found in Marx' letter to Annenkow, the *Manifesto*, the 1859 Preface, *Capital* and *Anti-Dühring*, to cite just those obvious examples. They all offer explanations to the effect that agency will not fail to do so, previous transformations are explained in terms of fettering, and, explicitly or implicitly, revolutionary responses to it. And the confidence in the expected transition from capitalism to socialism and eventually classless communist society is argued in terms of the effects of capitalist development in themselves uniting, steeling and organising the capitalist working class. But no adequate *proof* that *all* cases of the fettering of the development of the productive forces can be trusted to be overcome in this way, or for that matter that the capitalist relations of production will indeed, with all their negative effects, fetter that development, is offered. That is, the confidence that the class capacities of the class with an interest in the realisation of the potential development of the productive forces will be adequate – and utilised – to overcome its fettering by the relations of production and, in the case of capitalism, that the isolation of class struggle will be overcome, is not supported by any cogent argument. In any case, the demonstration why this confidence is well-founded must be offered in the case of every *specific* mode of production, every *specific* integument which has to be burst asunder because no longer compatible with the already developed productive forces.[31]

---

[31] Cf. Marx & Engels, *Manifest der Kommunistischen Partei*, p. 467 ff.

The conception of the dialectic of forces and relations of production as the motive power of historical development and transformations is the major problem with Marx' and Engels' historical materialism, *firstly* because it is in effect informing their entire intellectual trajectory from the mid-1840s;[32] *secondly* because their expectations and predictions about the inevitability of the transition from capitalism to socialism and eventually classless communist society are based on it; and *thirdly* because the failure of these expectations and predictions to come true leaves a yawning gap in their historical materialism in terms of the *strategy* for the accomplishment of this transition as well as in terms of *explaining* that very failure and the actual historical development of capitalism.

The critique of Marx' and Engels' historical materialism made by this writer turns on the weakness of this conception and hence of their corresponding idea of the process of historical development as ruled by laws comparable to those of natural development and their predictions of the transition from capitalism to socialism and eventually classless communist society as inevitable. It emphasises the tension between this conception and that of human agents as the makers of their own history (under the given and inherited circumstances with

---

[32] Marx & Engels, *Die deutsche Ideologie*, p. 69-77, p. 424, Marx & Engels, *Manifest der Kommunistischen Partei*, section I, Marx, *Das Kapital*, 1, ch. 24.7, and Engels, *Anti-Dühring*, Part III, ch. II. Further evidence of this conception and Marx' and Engels' predictions about the inevitable transition from capitalism to socialism and eventually classless communist society (and attempts to deny the latter) is cited in Gram-Jensen, *Structure, Agency and Theory*, Part One, ch. 2-3 and Appendix Three; the second essay in Gram-Jensen: *Experience and Historical Materialism*; the first, second and seventh essay in Gram-Jensen: *A Critique of Mau: Mute Compulsion and Other Essays*; and the second essay in Gram-Jensen: *A Revised Historical Materialism*.

which they are directly confronted)[33] and argues that *the inter-action between social circumstances and agency* should be substituted for the dialectic of forces and relations of production as the supposed motive power of historical development and trans-formations, with the process of historical development con-ceived as *open-ended* within the limits imposed by the given so-cial circumstances.

The Tension in Marx' and Engels' Historical Material-ism.

Biological development is a wholly unconscious, non-teleo-logical process; social/historical development depends on agents' *conscious* relating to, and handling, their "lived" reality, thus, through this practice, interacting with their social cir-cumstances. Hence *intentions* are part of this process, although they may not be actualised.

The tension in Marx' and Engels' historical materialism, as it developed over time, is basically a matter of the irreducibility of the interaction between social circumstances and agency to a process ruled by quasi-natural *laws* of development de-termining the will, consciousness and intentions of agents, that is, a quasi-natural process of development comparable to that of the development of species. The tension is due to the fact that while the specificity of the historical development of human society: that human beings relate consciously to their own life activity, is recognised in an explicit contradistinction to animals, there is *also* a marked tendency in Marx and En-gels to posit *laws* of historical development in effect reducing

---

[33] Marx, *The Eighteenth Brumaire of Louis Bonaparte*, p. 146 (*MEW*, 8, p. 115). Marx & Engels, *Die heilige Familie*, p. 98, *Die deutsche Ideologie*, p. 45. Cf. Mills' description of this fundamental ambiguity as "the unresolved tension in Marx's work – and in history itself: the ten-sion of humanism and determinism, of human freedom and histor-ical necessity." (Mills, p. 99).

it to a (quasi-)natural process comparable to natural/biological development.

It is characteristic that in *Capital*, vol. 1, in the Afterword to the second edition of which we find Marx' approving quotation from the Russian reviewer the point of which is precisely that "the social movement" is such "a process of natural history ruled by laws that are not only independent of the will, consciousness and intentions of people, but on the contrary determine [*bestimmen*] their will, consciousness and intentions",[34] Marx also states that the proletariat will be disciplined, united and organised by the mechanism of the capitalist process of production, the monopoly on capital becoming a fetter on the mode of production, and that the capitalist integument will be burst asunder[35]: a passage echoing the first section of the *Manifesto*, and with a footnote in which the prediction that the fall of the bourgeoisie and the victory of the proletariat are equally inevitable (Marx & Engels, *Manifest der Kommunistischen Partei*, p. 474) is quoted.

A revolutionary-socialist working-class response to the development of capitalism, and the capacity of the working class to actually *succeed* in effecting the transition from capitalism to socialism and eventually classless communist society, must be presumed to be guaranteed by the laws assumed to be ruling social development, but it is not obvious that either the existence of such laws or the inevitability of this transition have been demonstrated either theoretically or by the course of history.

What is certain is that the irreducibility of human agency as a crucial factor in historical development is in effect retracted by the positing of the (quasi-natural) *laws* ruling this

---

[34] Marx, *Das Kapital*, 1, p. 26.
[35] Marx, *Das Kapital*,1, p. 790-791.

development, part of the context of which is the conception of the dialectic of forces and relations of production as the motive power of historical development and transformations found in Marx' and Engels' texts from the mid-1840s[36] and on. As the final words of the second essay in *A Revised Historical Materialism* go:

> The discernible drift in Marx and Engels' historical materialism towards an explanation of historical development and transformations in terms of laws of social/historical development of which agency is a function, clashing with their emphasis on human agents as the makers of their own history (under given and inherited circumstances), is evidence of the tension between this conception of agency on the one hand and that of the dialectic of forces and relations of production as the motive power of historical development and transformations on the other. While the latter conception should certainly be abandoned, the strategic gap it leaves behind urgently needs to be filled.[37]

Engels' Parallelograms of Forces.
Engels' hypothesis on the parallelograms of forces and its context in the letter in which Engels outlines it are as follows:

> [.....]. According to the materialist conception of history, the *ultimately* determining element in history is the production and reproduction of real life. More than this neither Marx nor I have ever asserted. Hence if somebody twists this into saying that the economic element is the *only* determining one, he transforms that

---

[36] Marx & Engels, *Die deutsche Ideologie*, p. 69-77, p. 424. Cf. Marx, *A Contribution to the Critique of Political Economy*, p. 20-22 (*MEW*, 13, p. 8-9).

[37] Gram-Jensen, *A Revised Historical Materialism*, p. 184-185.

proposition into a meaningless, abstract, senseless phrase. The economic situation is the basis, but the various elements of the superstructure – political forms of the class struggle and its results, to wit: constitutions established by the victorious class after a successful battle, etc., juridical forms, and even the reflexes of all these actual struggles in the brains of the participants, political, juristic, philosophical theories, religious views and their further development into systems of dogmas – also exercise their influence upon the course of the historical struggles and in many cases preponderate in determining their *form*. There is an interaction of all these elements in which, amid all the endless host of accidents (that is, of things and events whose inner interconnection is so remote or so impossible of proof that we can regard it as non-existent, as negligible) the economic movement finally asserts itself as necessary. Otherwise the application of the theory to any period of history would be easier than the solution of a simple equation of the first degree.

We make our history ourselves, but, in the first place, under very definite assumptions and conditions. Among these the economic ones are ultimately decisive. But the political ones, etc., and indeed even the traditions which haunt human minds also play a part, although not the decisive one. The Prussian state also arose and developed from historical, ultimately economic, causes. But it could scarcely be maintained without pedantry that among the many small states of North Germany, Brandenburg was specifically determined by economic necessity to become the great power embodying the economic, linguistic and, after the Reformation, also the religious difference between North and South, and not by other element[s] as well (above all by its entanglement with Poland, owing to its possession of Prussia, and hence with international political relations – which were indeed also decisive in the formation of the Austrian dynastic power). Without making oneself ridiculous it would be a difficult thing to explain in terms of economics the existence of every small state in Germany, past and present, or the origin of the High German consonant permutations, which widened the geographic partition wall formed by the mountains from the Sudetic range to the Taunus to form a regular fissure across all Germany.

In the second place, however, history is made in such a way that the final result always arises from conflicts between many individual wills, of which each in turn has been made what it is by a host of particular conditions of life. Thus there are innumerable intersecting forces, an infinite series of parallelograms of forces which give rise to one resultant – the historical event. This may again itself be viewed as the product of a power which works as a whole *unconsciously* and without volition. For what each individual wills is obstructed by everyone else, and what emerges is something that no one willed. Thus history has proceeded hitherto in the manner of a natural process and is essentially subject to the same laws of motion. But from the fact that the wills of individuals – each of whom desires what he is impelled to by his physical constitution and external, in the last resort economic, circumstances (either his own personal circumstances or those of society in general) – do not attain what they want, but are merged into an aggregate mean, a common resultant, it must not be concluded that they are equal to zero. On the contrary, each contributes to the resultant and is to this extent included in it.[38]

The fundamental problem with this argument on the infinite series of parallelograms of forces is that the conflicting individual wills are *in effect*, in spite of Engels' disclaimer that "it must not be concluded that they are equal to zero", that each individual will contributes to the resultant and is to this extent included in it, supposed to *cancel out*, so that what emerges is not only something that no one willed, but history may also be assumed to proceed in the manner of a natural process and essentially subject to the same laws of motion. Engels is not just arguing that historical outcomes are frequently if not always something which neither of the struggling groups and individuals wanted; that would not be fatal, although the point may be exaggerated. What he argues *is* in effect that the conflicting wills of the actors somehow cancel out and thus merges into "a common resultant" the effect of which is, again in an unexplained way, that historical development proceeds in the manner of a natural process and is essentially [*wesentlich*] subject to the same laws of motion.

In contradistinction to the idea of human agents' will, consciousness and intentions being determined by laws of historical development, Engels' conception of parallelograms of forces leaves room for agents' articulation of their experiences of and responses to their "lived" reality, and hence for their will, consciousness and intentions, but at the same time he declares the wills of human actors powerless by positing their cancelling out. Which leaves room for quasi-natural laws of motion to make historical development proceed in the

---

[38] Engels, "Engels an Joseph Bloch in Königsberg, 21./22. September 1890", p. 463-464 (translation from Marx & Engels, *Selected Correspondence*, p. 417-418); cf. *Ludwig Feuerbach und der Ausgang der klassischen deutschen Philosophie*, p. 296 ff.

manner of a natural process, but may make it possible for Engels to uphold the claim made in *Anti-Dühring* that,

> With the seizing of the means of production by society, production of commodities is done away with, and, simultaneously, the mastery of the product over the producer. Anarchy in social production is replaced by plan-conforming, conscious organization. The struggle for individual existence disappears. Then for the first time man, in a certain sense, is finally marked off from the rest of the animal kingdom, and emerges from mere animal conditions of existence into really human ones. The whole sphere of the conditions of life which environ man, and which have hitherto ruled man, now comes under the dominion and control of man, who for the first time becomes the real, conscious lord of nature, because he has now become master of his own social organization. The laws of his own social action, hitherto standing face to face with man as laws of nature foreign to, and dominating him, will then be used with full understanding, and so mastered by him. Man's own social organization, hitherto confronting him as a necessity imposed by nature and history, now becomes the result of his own free action. The extraneous objective forces that have hitherto governed history pass under the control of man himself. Only from that time will man himself, with full consciousness, make his own history – only from that time will the social causes set in movement by him have, in the main and in a constantly growing measure, the results intended by him. It is the ascent of man from the kingdom of necessity to the kingdom of freedom.[39]

---

[39] Engels, *Anti-Dühring*, p. 335-336 (*MEW*, 20, p. 264).

There is no doubt that Marx shared this notion that with the abolition of class divisions, human agents win the control over their own social existence, thus closing the prehistory of human society.[40] The question about how to accomplish it if no laws of historical can be trusted to make it inevitable remains, however. And in any case Engels' idea of the parallelograms of power cancelling out suffers from certain weaknesses, the most fundamental of which is the logical inconsistency of it: if the wills of individuals are *not* equal to zero, agency must have *some* degree of causal efficacy – but if human wills, which are not reducible to effects of the laws of motion to which history is subjected, *do* influence the course of history in any *real* sense, then history does *not* proceed "in the manner of a natural process and [.....] essentially subject to the same laws of motion". Engels is in effect trying to have it both ways, and thus ends up in a logical dead end.

The mere fact that conflicting wills pull in different directions does not mean that the outcome of the conflict between them will not be affected by the precise nature of the aims involved or by differences of *strength* between the collective and individual actors involved, whether for structural or historical reasons. For one thing, the structural determination of the state means that some wills are more likely than others to be successful in a variety of contexts; but other wills may still be causally effective in various contexts, pushing events in another direction than they would otherwise have taken. And in any event, given that the articulation of wills (experiences and responses, strategies and tactics) is irreducible to effects of the developmental logic of the structure, some ways in which wills are fought for will be more effective than others, so that equal success or failure of the given conflicting wills cannot be taken for granted. If agents are supposed to react

---

[40] Marx, *A Contribution to the Critique of Political Economy*, p. 21-22 (*MEW*, 13, p. 9).

consciously to their own existence, and handle it accordingly, and this is the reason why there is such a thing as historical, rather than merely biological, development of the human species,[41] does it make no difference *how* they react to it and handle it? Whether they articulate rational or irrational responses to it? Whether they adopt rational or irrational strategies and tactics in order to handle it? Do the laws assumed to rule historical development assure that human choices, and consequent actions, makes no real difference to its actual course? The logic of Engels' argument certainly tends towards the reduction of agents to mere supports of these laws and the historical development they rule. And conversely, if actors' choice of one line of action rather than another *can* make a real difference (one line being more effective than another and/or aiming at another goal), the assumption that conflicting wills are bound to produce an outcome which is essentially determined by laws comparable to those ruling natural processes is wrong. Which it certainly seems to be.

It is perfectly realistic to assume that historical developments by and large eventuate from conflicting wills and actors' handling of such conflicts, and that the final results of these conflicts, the tug-of-war between the involved actors taking place in given circumstances, will rarely be identical with the will of any of these actors. But that does not mean that their specific wills and the specific ways in which they handle the conflict cannot make any real difference to the outcome. This may be illustrated by assuming a conflict between three actors, 1, 2 and 3 – they could be three parties representing e. g. feudal, capitalist and working class in some given social formation. Each of them may adopt various specific objectives in terms of politics and economics, or international politics, compromises between these objectives being more or less easy to

---

[41] Marx, *Early Writings*, p. 328-329 (*MEW*, Ergänzungsband, erster Teil, p. 516-517).

arrange. And each of the actors may adopt a more or less uncompromising or conciliatory line towards one or both of the other two: the feudal class may, for example, try to make advances to the working class in order to counteract the capitalist one, and/or the capitalist class may try to make advances to the working class in order to counteract the feudal class – depending on the actual lines of conflict (e. g. the extension of the suffrage, industrial and agrarian politics, taxation, etcetera). And the working class may adopt a revolutionary, gradualist or reformist line, and try to make deals with either the feudal or the capitalist class on different issues. And so on.

If, then, actor 1 chooses line A rather than line B, actor 2 chooses line C rather than line D, and actor 3 chooses line E rather than line F, the result(s) must be assumed to be likely to be different from that which would have eventuated from their choice of B, D and F. Or, alternatively, if such choices are assumed to make no difference, the implication is that the wills of the actors do *not* make any real difference, and human agents are *not* the makers of their own history (under the given and inherited circumstances with which they are directly confronted).[42]

In other words, assuming that the conflicts between the many individual (and collective) wills make history proceed in the manner of a natural process and subjected to the same laws of motion as natural processes implies that human agency is essentially ineffective, unable to make any *real* difference to the course of history. But historical outcomes being (always or usually) something that no one willed is not the same thing as human wills and agency being unable to make any real difference to them. And consequently, history *cannot* be taken to

---

[42] Cf. Marx, *The Eighteenth Brumaire of Louis Bonaparte*, p. 146 (*MEW*, 8, p. 115).

be reducible the outcomes of, or ruled by, laws comparable to those of natural processes.

But if so, what is Engels' basis for assuming that agents' wills will *in effect* cancel out? Nothing, it seems: the assumption seems to be a mere postulate, an *ad hoc* reason offered why laws comparable to those ruling natural developments can be assumed to rule historical development. *Ad hoc* in the sense that it is not supported by any historical experience, its only merit being that it offers the wanted explanation.[43] Engels does not, in his letter to Bloch, spell out the laws of motion supposed to rule historical development, but there is no reason not to believe that he was thinking of the dialectic of forces and relations of production conceived as the motive power of historical development and transformations, and along the same line as in *Anti-Dühring, Die Entwicklung des Sozialismus von der Utopie zur Wissenschaft* and *Ludwig Feuerbach und der Ausgang der klassischen deutschen Philosophie*.

In *A Revised Historical Materialism*, it was noted that, "Marx' solution as sketched in the Afterword to the second edition of *Capital* is, if it is to be taken literally, the most radical and, for the said purpose, the most effective, eradicating any authentical articulation by agents of their own ends. Thus, it is also the one which most emphatically eliminates agents as the makers of their own history in any real sense, reducing them to mere supports of the laws determining their will, consciousness and intentions as part of the determination of historical development."[44] The tension – and problem – in Marx' and Engels' historical materialism in this context consists, firstly, in the fact that Marx and Engels *do* maintain that

---

[43] Cf. Koch, p. 391-393, p. 572.

[44] Gram-Jensen, *A Revised Historical Materialism*, p. 42-43; the precise formulations referred to are, of course, those approvingly quoted from a Russian reviewer by Marx (Marx, *Das Kapital*, 1, p. 25-27; cf. p. 25-28, passim).

human agents make their own history (under their given and inherited circumstances)[45], whereas the assumption that the social movement is "a process of natural history ruled by laws that are not only independent of the will, consciousness and intentions of people, but on the contrary determine their will, consciousness and intentions"[46] in effect reduces human agency to a simple effect of the said laws, without any causal efficacy of its own – a reduction also implied by Engels' idea of individual wills cancelling out. And secondly, that this reduction does not seem to constitute a useful basis of historical explanation, as well as its logical implication being that any attempts – such as those of Marx and Engels themselves – to make the working class aware of its class interest in the transition from capitalism to socialism and eventually classless communist society and further its organisation around this interest are ultimately meaningless. If the wills, consciousness and intentions of agents are determined by laws similar to those ruling natural processes, then any attempt to make a difference to the course of the social movement is futile, although of course explainable as an effect of those same laws.[47]

---

[45] Or, as Marx emphasises in his *Economic and Philosophical Manuscripts* of 1844, human agents are conscious beings relating consciously to their own lives (Marx, *Early Writings*, p. 328 (*MEW*, Ergänzungsband, erster Teil, p. 516)).

[46] Marx, *Das Kapital*, 1, p. 26.

[47] Another implication is the impossibility of rational argument on the determinist assumption that "everything that happens has a cause and could not have happened differently unless something in the cause or causes had also been different" (Carr, p. 93), because "according to this view our thinking is determined in one context, the causal one, to such a degree that no mobility remains in the other, the logical one; and all our thinking and arguing against each other presupposes this mobility in consideration of correctness." (Knud Grue-Sørensen, *Studier over refleksivitet*, J. H. Schultz Forlag, København 1950, p. 191, quoted from Favrholt, p. 283; cf. Favrholt, p. 159, p. 281-283; and section d of the third essay in Gram-Jensen, *Experience and Historical Materialism*).

It might be argued that the precision of the determination of the will, consciousness and intentions of agents by the laws ruling the social movement is not specified by either the Russian reviewer or Marx: it may be assumed to leave some room for non-determined agency to make a real difference. But if so, how can the social be considered a process of natural history ruled by laws that are not only independent of the will, consciousness and intentions of people, but on the contrary determine their will, consciousness and intentions? It is of course true that Marx and Engels have expressed themselves in less determinist terms, but the tension between agents as the makers of their own history under given and inherited circumstances (the economy being determining in the *final* instance) and a (lawed) process of natural history of the kind suggested by the words of the Afterword is unmistakable. It seems reasonable to say that it was never resolved by Marx and Engels.

As noted, one finds this ambivalence and consequent tension in historical materialism in Marx' and Engels' texts from the mid-1840s and on: on the one hand human agents are found cast in the role as, precisely, *agents*, actors driving historical development forwards by pursuing their own ends[48] in response to their experiences of their "lived" reality; on the other hand, historical development advancing according to (quasi-natural) laws determining the will, consciousness and intentions of people. With the latter, the confidence in the inevitability of the eventual transition from capitalism to socialism and eventually classless communist society presumed to be guaranteed by the dialectic of forces and relations of production which is conceived as the motive power of historical development and transformations only leaves room

[48] Marx & Engels, *Die heilige Familie*, p. 98; cf. *Die deutsche Ideologie*, p. 45.

for the possibility of shortening and alleviating the birthpangs of the process by means of agents' *knowledge* about these "natural laws" of social development.[49]

In spite of this formula, the two lines of thought are mutually exclusive, and if we are to understand the dynamic of historical development and transformations, and thus be able to handle it as effectively as possible, we should opt for the conception of historical development as the interaction between social circumstances and agency.[50]

Further Remarks on Marx' and Engels' Historical Materialism.

The very simplicity of the trajectory of types of society implied by the conception of the dialectic of forces and relations of production as the motive power of historical development and transformations seems to be a weakness of the conception: it is a reductive conception of historical causation and development. The potential effects of relations *between* social formations suggested by Marx' and Engels' references to the historical transitions from one type of society to another caused by foreign conquest[51] suggests a potentially more complex story than that implied by the dialectic of forces and relations of production, just as *agency*, human agents' handling of their "lived" reality with all its conditions and characteristics at the various points in time and space would seem to hold the potential for larger variations than just the alleviation

---

[49] Marx, *Das Kapital*, 1, p. 15-16.

[50] Sørensen puts this point well in *Den europæiske deltagelseskrise*, p. 70-71, but unfortunately fails to point out that the conception of the dialectic of forces and relations of production as the motive power of historical development and transformations is not only found in the tradition of the II. International, but also, and centrally, in Marx and Engels.

[51] Marx & Engels, *Die deutsche Ideologie*, p. 23-24; *Manifest der Kommunistischen Partei*, p. 462.

and shortening (or the opposite) of the birthpangs of the new type of society. The open-endedness of a more complex historical development is also, it would seem, suggested by the development since the beginning of the 20th century, including the rise, development and fall of societies of "real existing socialism".[52]

The positing of quasi-natural laws of historical development determining the will, consciousness and intentions of agents effectively amounts to an attempt to eliminate the element of open-endedness and unpredictability of historical development implied by human *agency* – an attempt which, as suggested, is not supported by the historical record.[53] Whereas the isolation of class struggle seems to be accountable for in terms of the interaction between social circumstances and agency as the motive power of historical development and transformations: this assumed motive power of historical development and transformations does not, to be sure, imply some definite direction or terminus of historical development in terms of which it may be falsified or confirmed by the historical record *so far*; but it does seem able to *make sense of* this record, to make it *understandable* as an effect of the interaction between social circumstances and agency.

---

[52] If we accept, as we should because of its peculiar mechanism of exploitation, that "real existing socialism" was/is neither capitalism nor a stage of transition to classless communist society, it is squarely inconsistent with Marx' and Engels' expectations and predictions in e. g. the *Manifesto*, the 1859 Preface, *Capital* (especially vol. 1, ch. 24.7) and *Anti-Dühring*.

[53] Strange to say, Marx does not seem to have been struck by the contradiction between the conception of the dialectic of forces and relations of production as the motive power of historical development and transformations on the one hand and his own sketch of the changeless Asiatic mode of production (Marx, *Das Kapital*, 1, p. 378-379) on the other (cf. Cohen, p. 386).

Historical development is caused by human agents' active relating to and handling their "lived" reality – but this also tells against the idea of the predictability of historical development, because human beings' future consciousness, ideas, experiences, responses and actions seem unpredictable *and* have implications for the future course of history.

If we exclude divine intervention and plan, there is only human agency to account for the fact of human history, social development. There are, of course, conditions and limits to the possible which are determinants of historical development, including the historically and ecologically given conditions and limits. But there would still be no (pre)history of human society at all without the interaction between social circumstances and agency.

Hence the laws supposed to rule historical development and transformations and determine the will, consciousness and intentions of agents may fairly be considered a quasi- or pseudo-religious element inadvertently introduced into Marx' and Engels' historical materialism by means of their turning Hegel's dialectics upside down.[54] Indeed, the positing of such laws does not seem very different from the positing of a divine will or order. The introduction of Darwin's theory on the origin of species[55] is a doubtful step forward: historical development and transformations is *not* a process comparable to that of species, which is, to be sure, not teleological but does not include any conscious element, nor a predictable direction.[56] And in any event the belief that the (pre)history of

---

[54] Marx, *Das Kapital*, 1, p. 27.
[55] Engels, "Engels an Marx in London, 11. oder 12. Dezember 1859". Marx, "Marx an Ferdinand Lasalle in Berlin, 16. Januar 1861", p. 578.
[56] Cf. Darwin, p. 118-119.

human society has a predictable terminus (even if not a *telos*) was not abandoned.[57]

One may ask why the tension in Marx' and Engels' historical materialism did not make them abandon the idea of history being ruled by quasi-natural laws determining the will, consciousness and intentions of human agents. Apart from the obvious attractiveness of the idea that the supersession of capitalism by socialism and eventually classless communist society is inevitable because an effect of these laws, the reason is probably that in their time understanding some process or field of enquiry meant establishing the laws ruling it. As Carr wrote,

> [.....]. Throughout the eighteenth and nineteenth centuries, scientists assumed that laws of nature – Newton's laws of motion, the law of gravitation, Boyle's law, the law of evolution, and so forth – had been discovered and definitely established, and that the business of the scientist was to discover and establish more such laws from observed facts. The word 'law' came down trailing clouds of glory from Galilei and Newton. Students of society, consciously or unconsciously desiring to assert the scientific status of their studies, adopted the same language and believed themselves to be following the same procedure. The political economists seem to have been the first in the field with Gresham's law, and Adam Smith's laws of the market. Burke appealed to 'the laws of commerce, which are

---

[57] Here one may in fact agree with Laclau & Mouffe's remarks in *Hegemony and Socialist Strategy*, p. 20, p. 94-95, p. 123-124, although certainly not with their inferences from this weakness of Marx' and Engels' historical materialism. Cf. on Hegel Kaufmann, p. 137, p. 156 (quoted in Gram-Jensen, *Structure, Agency and Theory*, p. 998), and on Hegel's conception of history and its influence on Marx Cohen, ch. 1, especially p. 1, p. 26-27.

the laws of nature, and consequently the Laws of God'. Malthus propounded a law of population; Lasalle an iron law of wages; and Marx in the preface to *Capital* claimed to have discovered 'the economic law of motion of modern society'.[58]

In this context, it relevant to touch on Carr's definition and defence of determinism,

> [.....] which I will define – I hope, uncontroversially – as the belief that everything that happens has a cause and causes, and could not have happened differently unless something in the cause or causes had also been different. Determinism is a problem not of history, but of all human behaviour. The human being whose actions have no cause and are therefore undetermined is as much an abstraction as the individual outside society whom we discussed in a previous lecture. Professor Popper's assertion that 'everything is possible in human affairs' is either meaningless or false. Nobody in ordinary life believes or can believe this. The axiom that everything has a cause is a condition of our capacity to understand what is going on around us.[59]

Now, one does not have to accept Popper's assertion that, "[.....]. Indeed, it is necessary to recognise as one of the principles of any unprejudiced view of politics that everything is possible in human affairs" in a literal sense in order to doubt about the absolute validity of Carr's position. Popper's next words, however, refer to the discussion of laws assumed to rule historical development and transformations: "and more particularly that no conceivable development can be excluded on the grounds that it may violate the so-called tendency of

---

[58] Carr, p. 57-58.
[59] Carr, p. 93-94.

human progress, or any other of the alleged laws of 'human nature'."[60], although one might wonder whether *any* developments can be considered *in*conceivable if it is *literally* true that everything is possible in human affairs.

The question of strict determinism is dealt with in *Experience and Historical Materialism*,[61] but is so closely related to that of historical *predictions* that it is relevant here too. Carr himself noted that the notion of determinism as he defines it has been challenged by modern physics, but leaves the question open "[.....] whether the indeterminacy of modern physics resides in the nature of the universe, or is merely an index of our own hitherto imperfect understanding of it".[62] But as argued in *Experience and Historical Materialism*,

> [.....]. In fact strict determinism has been challenged both by quantum theory and by mutations: "unpredictable and discontinuous genetic 'leaps', sports or freaks, mostly unviable but occasionally of potential evolutionary advantage, upon which natural selection would operate", and thus obviously implying a deflection of the straight line of an unbroken chain of causal determination. The logical implication of their unpredictable occurrence and nature is that the future evolution of life is, at any given point in time, not completely predictable from its course until that very point, because it may be changed by some unforeseeable mutation.[63]

So, the evidence does, at least at the present, suggest that indeterminacy is a fact in some areas, and that prediction of

---

[60] Popper, *The Open Society and Its Enemies*, vol. 2, p. 197.
[61] Gram-Jensen, *Experience and Historical Materialism*, p. 172 ff.
[62] Carr, p.71-72; cf. p. 68-69.
[63] Gram-Jensen, *Experience and Historical Materialism*, p. 173; quotation from Hobsbawm, *The Age of Empire*, p. 255.

small-scale physical events is hence only possible in terms of their *probability*.[64] This is relevant to human consciousness and behaviour because mental processes must presumably involve processes at quantum level. This relationship between determination and indeterminacy has been described as follows:

> Even in a world that contains quantum uncertainty, macroscopic objects are determined to an extraordinary degree. Newton's laws of motion are deterministic enough to send men to the moon and back. Our Cogito model of the Macro Mind is large enough to ignore quantum uncertainty for the purpose of the reasoning will. The neural system is robust enough to insure that mental decisions are reliably transmitted to our limbs.
>
> Although it is limited by indeterminacy, we call this determinism, limited as it is in extremely small structures, "adequate determinism." The world is adequately determined to send men to the moon. The presence of quantum uncertainty leads philosophers to call the world "indetermined." But indeterminism is seriously misleading when most events are overwhelmingly "adequately determined."
>
> There is no problem imagining that the three traditional mental faculties of reason – perception, conception, and comprehension – are all carried on deterministically in a physical brain where quantum events do not interfere with normal operations.
>
> There is also no problem imagining a role for randomness in the brain in the form of quantum level noise.

---

[64] Cf. Pais, p. 21-22; cf. ch.s 10.c and 13.g.

Noise can introduce random errors into stored memories. Noise could create random associations of ideas during memory recall. This randomness may be driven by microscopic fluctuations that are amplified to the macroscopic level.

Our Macro Mind needs the Micro Mind for the free action items and thoughts in an Agenda of <u>alternative possibilities</u> to be de-liberated by the will. The random Micro Mind is the "free" in free will and the source of human <u>creativity</u>. The adequately determined Macro Mind is the "will" in free will that de-liberates, choosing actions for which we can be morally <u>responsible</u>.[65]

So much for the question of indeterminacy, or more precisely the question whether the articulation of human agents' will, consciousness and intentions is (theoretically if not in practice) predictable or open-ended. As for historical development, Marx and Engels stated in *Die Heilige Familie*, published 1845, that,

> [.....]. *History* does *nothing*, it "owns *no* immense riches", it "fights *no* battles"! On the contrary it is *man*, real, living man, who does, owns and fights all of it; it is definitely not "history" that uses man as a means of going through with *its* ends – as if it were a person apart – on the contrary it is *nothing* but the activity of man pursuing his own ends.[66]

And in *Die deutsche Ideologie*, written 1845-46:

---

[65] http://www.informationphilosopher.com/freedom/indeterminacy.html 18. November 2016.
[66] Marx & Engels, *Die heilige Familie*, p. 98.

History is nothing but the succession of the separate generations, each of which exploits the materials, the capital funds, the productive forces handed down to it by all preceding generations, and thus, on the one hand, continues the traditional activity in completely changed circumstances and, on the other, modifies the old circumstances with a completely changed activity. This can be speculatively distorted so that later history is made the goal of earlier history, e.g., the goal ascribed to the discovery of America is to further the eruption of the French Revolution. Thereby history receives its own special aims and becomes "a person ranking with other persons" [.....], while what is designated with the words "destiny", "goal", "germ", or "idea" of earlier history is nothing more than an abstraction formed from later history, from the active influence which earlier history exercises on later history.[67]

Here, "history" simply stands for the continuous process of interaction between social circumstances and agency. The social circumstances obtaining at any given point in time and space certainly condition it, and influence the will, consciousness and intentions of the human actors articulating their experiences of and responses to their "lived" reality, so that human actors cannot make their own history of their own free will, but have to do so on the given conditions and with the given materials handed down to them,[68] but the only aims involved are those of the human actors.

In the passages by the Russian reviewer Marx approvingly quoted in the Afterword to the second edition of *Capital*, the

---

[67] Marx & Engels, *Die deutsche Ideologie*, p. 45.
[68] Cf. Marx, *The Eighteenth Brumaire of Louis Bonaparte*, p. 146 (*MEW*, 8, p. 115).

point made in these earlier texts is reversed. In effect the reviewer conceives of history as precisely "a person apart" using human actors as a means of going through with *its* ends, as it does not only involve the conditions imposed by nature and the past, but is ruled by quasi-natural laws determining the will, consciousness and intentions of the human actors who are thus reduced to the mere supports or bearers of those laws.[69] This is in effect a *fetishisation* of history, of the process of historical development, in the sense defined by Cohen: "To make a fetish of something, or fetishize it, is to invest it with powers it does not in itself have."[70] Some might prefer the word *hypostatisation*, the conception of abstract concepts as persons, independent realities; but fetishisation seems to fit the case without suggesting too much. And the conception of history, the process of historical development suggested by the Russian reviewer and confirmed by Marx, is precisely the fetishisation of it which Marx and Engels warned against in *Die heilige Familie* and *Die deutsche Ideologie*, comparable to the reduction of human beings to the mere "*supports* or bearers of the guises (*Charactermasken*) assigned to them by the structure of relations in the social formation"[71] in Althusserian "structural Marxism" or to "'subject positions' within a discursive structure" in Laclau & Mouffe.[72] Such fetishisation, the conceiving of history as an actor, has been described by Thompson in his critique of Althusser:

> When the rules of a game have been read or inferred, we can then assign to each player his role or function in the game. He is (in terms of those rules) the game's

---

[69] Just as their wills or intentions are supposed to cancel out, thus allowing to let such laws rule historical development in Engels, "Engels an Joseph Bloch in Königsberg, 21./22. September 1890", p. 464.

[70] Cohen, p. 115.

[71] Althusser & Balibar, p. 320 (Brewster's Glossary, "Support").

[72] Laclau & Mouffe, *Hegemony and Socialist Strategy*, p. 115.

carrier, an element within its structure – a halfback or a goal-keeper. [.....]. But we must take the analogy further. For we do not go on to say that the goal-keeper is *being gamed*, or the capitalist is *being capitaled*. This is what Althusser, and, also, some structuralist anthropologists and sociologists, would wish us to say. Althusser offers us a pseudo-choice: either we must say that there are no rules but only a swarm of "individuals", or we must say that the rules *game* the players.

The difference between "playing" a game and being gamed illustrates the difference between rule-governed structuration of historical eventuation (within which men and women remain as subjects of their own history) and structural*ism*.[73]

To which Thompson added that, according to various forms of structuralism,

[.....] we are *structured* by social relations, *spoken* by pregiven linguistic structures, *thought* by ideologies, *dreamed* by myths, *gendered* by patriarchal sexual norms, *bonded* by affective obligations, *cultured* by *mentalités*, and *acted* by history's script. None of these ideas is, in origin, absurd, and some rest upon substantial additions to knowledge. But all slip, at a certain point, from sense to absurdity, and, in their sum, all arrive at a common terminus of unfreedom. Structuralism (this terminus of the absurd) is the ultimate product of self-alienated reason – "reflecting" the common-sense of the times – in which all human projects, endeavours, institutions, and even culture itself, appear to stand *outside* of men, to stand *against* men, as objective things, as the "Other" which, in its own turn, moves men around

---

[73] Thompson, *The Poverty of Theory and Other Essays*, p. 152-153.

as things. In the old days, the Other was then named "God" or Fate. Today it has been christened anew as Structure.[74]

Just as it is absurd and misleading to posit that a game *games* the players, it is absurd and misleading to posit that historical development *historises* the human actors responding to their "lived" reality.

This is not all there is to the question of the efficacy or otherwise of agency, however. In the first place, Marx' account of the struggles over the working day[75] strongly suggests the ability of workers to act strategically, and that this may make a real difference to the outcome of such struggles. This distance between the reviewer's (and, by virtue of his acknowledgement of it, Marx') exposition of "the dialectical method" and Marx' concrete, historical analysis indicates the tension in Marx' and Engels' historical materialism (as does their activism). Engels' argument about the parallelograms of forces resulting from agents' conflicting wills which consequently cancel out may be considered another attempt to bridge the gap between the idea of quasi-natural laws ruling historical development on the one hand and that of human actors as the makers of their own history on the other, even if it does not seem a convincing solution, or an adequate formula for the relationship between structural and historical analysis.

How can the idea of human agents – us – as the makers of their – our – own history be consistent with the conception of the dialectic of forces and relations of production as the motive power of historical development and transformations, and the inevitability of the transition from capitalism to socialism and eventually classless communist society

---

[74] Thompson, *The Poverty of Theory and Other Essays*, p. 153.
[75] Marx, *Das Kapital*, 1, ch. 8.5-7.

guaranteed by laws of historical development determining human agents' – our – will, consciousness and intentions?

It cannot – by positing those quasi-natural laws the conception of the dialectic of forces and relations of production as the motive power of historical development and transformations, and that of the inevitability of the transition from capitalism to socialism and eventually classless communist society can be upheld; but the idea of human actors as the makers of their own history in any real sense is subverted – as human actors are in effect reduced to the mere supports or bearers of the will, consciousness and intentions imposed on them by the laws ruling historical development and transformations.

From *Die deutsche Ideologie* and onwards, there are a number of formulations in Marx' and Engels' texts which predict that the transition from capitalism to socialism is inevitable because the working class will be forced to accomplish it by the effects of the development of capitalism. There is no need to quote more than two, one from *Die deutsche Ideologie*, the other from *Anti-Dühring*:

> Finally, from the conception of history we have sketched we obtain these further conclusions: (1) In the development of productive forces there comes a stage when productive forces and means of intercourse are brought into being, which, under the existing relationships, only cause mischief, and are no longer productive but destructive forces (machinery and money); and connected with this a class is called forth, which has to bear all the burdens of society without enjoying its advantages, which, ousted from society, is forced into the most decided antagonism to all other classes; a class which forms the majority of all members of society, and from which emanates the

consciousness of the necessity of a fundamental revolution, the communist consciousness, which may, of course, arise among the other classes too through the contemplation of the situation of this class.[76]

Whilst the capitalist mode of production more and more completely transforms the great majority of the population into proletarians, it creates the power which, under penalty of its own destruction, is forced to accomplish this revolution. Whilst it forces on more and more the transformation of the vast means of production, already socialized, into state property, it shows itself the way to accomplishing this revolution. *The proletariat seizes political power and turns the means of production in the first instance into state property.*[77]

Passages such as these may be read as predictions from historical experience rather than deductions from supposed *laws* of historical development, predictions of human actors' articulation of their (experiences of and) responses to historical development rather than of the will, consciousness and intentions imposed by such supposed laws of historical development, and with the consequences derivable from those same laws. But both the Preface to the first edition of *Capital* and the Afterword to the second[78] and Engels' argument about parallelograms of forces in *Ludwig Feuerbach und der Ausgang*

---

[76] Marx & Engels, *Die deutsche Ideologie*, p. 69 (cf. p. 38-39, p. 424). Cf. Marx, "Marx an Pawel Wassiljewitsch Annenkow in Paris, 28. Dezember [1846]", p. 549, *Das Elend der Philosophie*, p. 140-141, *Das Kapital*, 1, p. 790-791.

[77] Engels, *Anti-Dühring*, p. 332 (*MEW*, 20, p. 261); cf. ibid., p. 189 (*MEW*, 20, p. 146-147).

[78] Marx, *Das Kapital*, 1, p. 12, p. 15-16, p. 25-27.

der klassischen deutschen Philosophie and his 1890 letter to Bloch[79] bear witness to the presence of the idea of quasi-natural laws ruling historical development, the consequent tension in Marx' and Engels' historical materialism and the failure to resolve it.

Part of the problem is what is meant, and should be meant, by "the economic element", "the production and reproduction", being the *ultimately* [*in letzter Instanz*] determining element in history".[80] It should be obvious that the question, "how much does the economic element determine" cannot be given any meaningful answer: the question is not *how much*, or precisely *what*, it determines, which cannot be established in any general sense anyway, but *in what way* it is "ultimately" the determining element in history. If it is supposed to determine the general course of history in the sense that human agency may determine various historical circumstances such as the rise to a major power of Brandenburg,[81] while the long-term development of human society, with the rise and development of modes of production and types of societies and the passing from one to the other, proceeds in the manner of a natural process and essentially subject to the same laws of motion, then Marx' admonition to workers to fight for the abolition of capitalism and wage-labour instead of for "a fair day's wage for a fair day's work"[82] may be considered meaningful in the sense that the birthpangs of the realm of freedom might be shortened and alleviated if workers heeded it, but futile if workers' will, consciousness and intentions are

---

[79] Engels, *Ludwig Feuerbach und der Ausgang der klassischen deutschen Philosophie*, p. 296 ff. "Engels an Joseph Bloch in Königsberg, 21./22. September 1890", p. 463-464.
[80] Engels, "Engels an Joseph Bloch in Königsberg, 21./22. September 1890", p. 463.
[81] Engels, "Engels an Joseph Bloch in Königsberg, 21./22. September 1890", p. 463-464.
[82] Marx, *Lohn, Preis und Profit*, p. 152.

determined by laws ruling the (quasi-)natural process of the development of societies. And in *Capital*, vol. 1, ch. 24.7, Marx *also* states, along with formulations suggesting predictions from historical experience, that, "But the capitalist production begets with the necessity [*Notwendigkeit*] of a natural process its own negation."[83]

Conversely, if human agency may make the difference between the maintenance or supersession of a mode of production and type of society, then the idea of the *inevitability* of this historical transformation found in Marx' and Engels' texts from the mid-1840s and on, cannot be maintained, just as the development of the (pre)history of human societies must then be considered a process of a kind fundamentally different from that of natural history, although of course emerging from, and intertwined with, the latter.

In any case, if the relationship between human agency and laws of historical development, and the notion of determination in the last instance, remain somewhat ambiguous in Marx' and Engels' historical materialism, the idea of the *inevitability* of the transition from capitalism to socialism and eventually classless communist society is maintained from the mid-1840s and on. And it is precisely these ideas, the conception of the dialectic of forces and relations of production as the motive power of historical development and transformations and the notion of historical development as a quasi-natural process ruled by (quasi-natural) laws, which have to be substituted by the conception of historical development as an open-ended process of a unique kind, the motive power of which is the interaction between social circumstances and agency.

---

83 Marx, *Das Kapital*, 1, p. 791.

Thus, in the final analysis, what is at the bottom of the tension in Marx' and Engels' historical materialism, and thus their assumption of the inevitability of the transition from capitalism to socialism and eventually classless communist society, is the obvious fact that this transition cannot take place unless accomplished by human agency, that is, by human actors. Hence the drift towards the positing of *laws* of historical development and transformations determining the will, consciousness and intentions of those actors – more specifically the proletariat – who are both *forced* to accomplish the transition (on pain of their own destruction) and *taught* how to accomplish it by capitalist development itself.

This might pass as a hypothesis which has not, however, so far been confirmed by actual historical development – a hypothesis resting, in effect, on the hypothesis sketched in the 15 sentences in the 1859 Preface. But it cannot be confirmed by structural analysis if this and historical analysis are, as argued below, *complementary*: any suggestion that the structural analysis of *Capital*, and in particular the conclusion on the historical tendency of capitalist accumulation, the prediction of *Capital*, vol. 1, ch. 24.7, is confirmed or even proved by the preceding analysis of capitalist accumulation, let alone the 1859 Preface, is circular. Only historical analysis can (at least up to the present moment) confirm it, but, again, *has not so far done so*.

The reduction of human agents to the mere supports or bearers of the character masks imposed on them by their positions in the relations of production is legitimate *in*, and for the purpose of, structural analysis, but cannot be transferred into *historical* analysis or argument: in real history, agency *cannot* be so reduced and therefore the process of historical development must be assumed to be open-ended: within limits to the possible set by the dominant capitalist mode of production and the capitalist type of society – but still open-ended. Hence the questions of class capacities and agents' articulation of their experiences of and responses to their "lived" reality cannot be ignored.

This does not, of course, detract from the value of Marx' major, and huge, feat, the analysis of the capitalist mode of production and capitalist exploitation in *Capital*, nor that of the vision of classless communist society, or that of the fundamental idea of a historical materialism as the basis for understanding society and history. But it does, again, leave a strategic gap in his and Engels' historical materialism because their conception of the dialectic of forces and relations of production as the motive power of historical development and transformations and their faith in the inevitability of the transition from capitalism to socialism and eventually classless communist society, based on that conception and on the idea of historical development as determined by quasi-natural laws guaranteeing this transition, seemed to promise that the problems of accomplishing it and how to organise an effectively classless communist society would be solved by the very process of historical development itself.

3. The Denial of Determinism in Marx and Engels.

The basic argument against the refusal to read Marx' and Engels' texts in a deterministic sense, that is, as sincerely predicting the inevitable transition from capitalism to socialism and eventually classless communist society (a prediction based on the conception of the dialectic of forces and relations of production as the motive power of historical development and transformations), a refusal which is grounded on the first two periods of section I of the Communist *Manifesto*, was made in the essay "Reading Marx" in *Experience and Historical Materialism*. It was more definite there than in *Structure, Agency and Theory*, which was written earlier, but published later, than *Experience and Historical Materialism*, and in which it was somewhat inconclusively stated that:

> [.....]. Another remark perhaps relevant to the relationship between determinism and activism, with the emphasis of the latter on the importance of organisation and the right practical line, is that in the *Manifesto* on historical class struggles having hitherto led to *either* a revolutionary transformation *or* the common ruin of the struggling classes (Marx & Engels, *Manifest der Kommunistischen Partei*, p. 462). This is obviously inconsistent with some of the passages quoted in the present text, including that in the *Manifesto* itself on the inevitable victory of the proletariat (ibid., p. 473-474), *if* – and *only* if – meant for capitalism too.[84]

Draper.

It is hard to say exactly when and by whom the denial of determinism in Marx and Engels was originally advanced, but one prominent instance of it is Draper's misinterpretation of the said two periods which run:

---

[84] Gram-Jensen, *Structure, Agency and Theory*, p.115, note 26.

63

The history of all hitherto existing society is the history of class struggles.

Freeman and slave, patrician and plebeian, lord and serf, guild-master and journeyman, in a word, oppressor and oppressed, stood in constant opposition to one another, carried on an uninterrupted, now hidden, now open fight, a fight that each time ended, either in a revolutionary reconstitution at large, or in the common ruin of the contending classes.[85]

In *The Adventures of the Communist Manifesto*, Draper argued that,

[.....]. Above all, this passage shows how mythical is the view that Marx believed in some sort of metaphysical "inevitability of socialism," according to which socialist victory is as fatefully predestined as, say, the salvation of Calvinist saints: a myth mostly based on a reading of Par. 60. On the contrary, society is faced with the alternatives later tagged "socialism or barbarism" – either a revolution that remakes society or the collapse of the old order to a lower level. Engels later repeated the alternative in *Anti-Dühring* (end of Pt. II, Chap. 2): the productive forces out of control, "are driving the whole of bourgeois society towards ruin, or revolution." Or (Pt. III, Chap. 2): the proletariat has to accomplish its revolution "under penalty of its own destruction" if it fails to do so. The great example in everyone's mind of the "common ruin of the contending classes" was the revolutionless disintegration of the society of the Roman Empire into "Caesarism" and a "dark" age. (See KMTR 1:465.) In contemporary

---

[85] Marx & Engels, *Manifest der Kommunistischen Partei*, p. 462.

Europe, "class struggle and rivalry in conquest have tuned up the public power to such a pitch that it threatens to swallow the whole of society and even the state," thought Engels (*Origin of the Family*, Chap. 9). The Manifesto makes it clear that the fate of society will be decided as usual by social struggle, not metaphysics.[86]

He also dismissed the prediction at the end of section I of the *Manifesto* that, "What the bourgeoisie therefore produces, above all, are its own grave-diggers. Its fall and the victory of the proletariat are equally inevitable",[87] writing that,

(4) INEVITABILITY. Upon the shaky foundation of this paragraph's last sentence has been built a whole theory, repeated from tome to tome, according to which Marx held a metaphysical theory about the "inevitability of socialism." But--

(a) This alleged theory flies in the face of the strong statement earlier about the alternatives before society: social revolution or else "the common ruin of the contending classes." (See Par.8/3, which cites further evidence.)

(b) The phrase °equally inevitable° (used by the A.E.T. in all innocence) is nonsense if it is taken literally, like "equally perfect." [.....]. The word used here for °inevitable° (°unvermeidlich°) is the ordinary German word (unavoidable,' 'necessitated') which often, as in English, conveys nothing more than high hope and confidence in a hortatory context. The same applies to the use of 'inevitably' in the Marx-Engels preface to the Russian edition of the Manifesto. If a philosophic

---

[86] Draper, *The Adventures of the Communist Manifesto*, p. 210; cf. *Karl Marx's Theory of Revolution*, I, p. 465-466.
[87] Marx & Engels, *Manifest der Kommunistischen Partei*, p. 474.

Theory of Inevitability were to be assigned to every writer who has used *unvermeidlich* in the same way, the history of thought would have to be rewritten. In practice, the *unvermeidlich* is counterposed to the accidental, in order to stress that a phenomenon obeys definite laws and is the outcome of causes that can be examined; it implies a scientific attitude to causation, not a metaphysical one.[88]

Apart from the somewhat rigged contrast Draper posits with a choice between social struggle and "metaphysics", and the fact that the context makes it rather obvious that *unvermeidlich* at the end of the section should be read as "inevitable", there are some points suggesting that Draper's argument is untenable. Firstly, if Marx and Engels wanted to make a strong statement to the effect that the struggle for socialism may end *either* victoriously *or* with the common ruin of the contending classes, why would they proclaim the inevitability of the victory of the proletariat at the end of the section?

Secondly, the latter statement concludes an argumentation over a number of pages turning on the dialectic of forces and relations of production as the motive power of historical development and transformations, according to which the feudal fetters on the development of the productive forces had to be burst asunder, and were burst asunder, and that now the same goes for the capitalist mode of production which is consequently doomed to perish at the hands of the proletariat;[89] whereas the words about the common ruin of the contending classes is merely a bald statement of fact made in a few lines.

---

[88] Draper, *The Adventures of the Communist Manifesto*, p. 243. The reference to Par.8/3 is to the former passage quoted above.
[89] Marx & Engels, *Manifest der Kommunistischen Partei*, p. 467-474.

Thirdly, these words about the common ruin of the contending classes mention freeman and slave, patrician and plebeian, lord and serf and guild-master and journeyman – but *not* bourgeois and proletarian. The contradiction between the two statements turns out, then, to be nonexistent: the words about the common ruin of the contending classes do *not* pertain to bourgeoisie and proletariat, but to pre-capitalist classes only.

In *Experience and Historical Materialism*, the conclusion that the words about the common ruin of the contending classes do *only* allude to *pre*-capitalist class struggles, *not* to that between bourgeoisie and proletariat, was unequivocally drawn from this fact that, "the sentence on class struggle in history mentions freeman and slave, patrician and plebeian, lord and serf, guild-master and journeyman, *not* capitalist and proletarian.".[90] And the precise plausible meaning of the words "the common ruin of the contending classes" in the *Manifesto* was identified for the first time in the essay "In Defence of *Structure, Agency and Theory*" in *A Critique of Mau:* Mute Compulsion *and Other Essays*.[91] One may add that if these words do indeed refer to conquest and the subsequent imposition of new relations of production, this in effect suggests a limit to the extent to which historical development and transformations are ruled by laws comparable to those ruling natural development: conquest may in some cases outdo the asserted dialectic of forces and relations of production (the idea of which as the motive power of historical development and transformations is, of course, rejected as part of the present argument in any case).

---

[90] Gram-Jensen, *Experience and Historical Materialism*, p. 73-74, p. 320, note 148.
[91] Gram-Jensen, *A Critique of Mau:* Mute Compulsion *and Other Essays*, p. 171 (cf. p. 206, note 331); cf. *A Revised Historical Materialism*, p. 134-136. Marx & Engels, *Die deutsche Ideologie*, p. 23-24.

Ellen Meiksins Wood.

In her essay "History or technological determinism?", Ellen Meiksins Wood demonstrates a decline of scholarship comparable to that of others denying the determinism in Marx' and Engels' historical materialism when asserting that,

> It is surely significant that in Marx's own accounts of historical transitions the development of productive forces plays little role as the primary motor. This is true even in his explanation of the transition from feudalism to capitalism. His most comprehensive accounts of pre-capitalist societies in the *Grundrisse*, and of the historical transition to capitalism – especially in the section on 'Primitive Accumulation' in *Capital* – do not invoke the development of productive forces as the motivating impulse of historical change. They are, in fact, based on the premise that what needs to be explained is precisely the origin of capitalism's distinctive drive to improve the forces of production.[92]

As pointed out in *A Critique of Mau:* Mute Compulsion *and Other Essays*,[93] this is simply wrong. Marx (alone or in company with Engels) *most explicitly* invokes the development of the productive forces, *and its fettering by the relations of production*, as "the motivating impulse of historical change": in *Die deutsche Ideologie*,[94] in his letter to Annenkow of 28 December 1842, and in *Das Elend der Philosophie*,[95] in the *Manifesto*, in the

---

[92] Meiksins Wood, p. 137.

[93] Gram-Jensen, *A Critique of Mau:* Mute Compulsion *and Other Essays*, p. 39-43; cf. p. 64-65. Gram-Jensen, *Structure, Agency and Theory*, Appendix Three quotes a number of passages predicting the inevitable transition from capitalism to socialism and eventually classless communist society.

[94] Marx & Engels, *Die deutsche Ideologie*, p. 22, p. 69-77, p. 424.

[95] Marx, "Marx an Pawel Wassiljewitsch Annenkow in Paris, 28. Dezember [1846]", p. 549; *Das Elend der Philosophie*, p. 140-141.

Grundrisse,[96] in the 1859 Preface to *A Contribution to the Critique of Political Economy*,[97] in *Das Kapital*, 1, ch. 24.7, in his letter to the editorial board of the *Otetschestwennyje Sapiski*,[98] in his drafts of an answer to Vera Zasulich.[99] To which one may add Engels' *Anti-Dühring* and the texts based on it, which Marx endorsed.[100] It is astounding, to say the least, that Meiksins Wood tries to dismiss this evidence as mere, and rare, "shorthand aphorisms" remarkable for "their poetic allusiveness and economy of expression", which, she hints (without presenting any evidence to that effect), are gainsaid by "the weight of his whole life's work and what it tells us about his theoretical principles."[101]

As for the critique of Mau, his *Mute Compulsion* contains much which is interesting, but his reading of Marx and Engels leaves much to be desired. How is it possible for him to fail to see Marx' predictions about the abolition of capitalism caused by the dialectic of forces and relations of production

---

[96] Marx, *Grundrisse*, p. 749-750. See the Appendix below for more passages in the *Grundrisse* to the same effect.

[97] Marx, *A Contribution to the Critique of Political Economy*, p. 21-22 (*MEW*, 13, p. 9).

[98] Marx, ["Brief an die Redaktion der "Otetschestwennyje Sapiski""], p. 108-111.

[99] Marx, ["Entwürfe einer Antwort auf den Brief von V. I. Sassulitsch"], p. 385-386, p. 390, p. 397-398.

[100] Marx, [Vorbemerkung zur französischen Ausgabe (1880)] in Engels: *Die Entwicklung des Sozialismus von der Utopie zur Wissenschaft*, p. 185.

[101] Meiksins Wood, p. 129; cf. the length at which the dialectic of forces and relations of production as "the motivating impulse of historical change" is argued in the *Manifesto* (Marx & Engels, *Manifest der Kommunistischen Partei*, section I), the 1859 Preface to *A Contribution to the Critique of Political Economy* (p. 21-22 (*MEW*, 13, p. 9)) and *Capital*, 1, ch. 24.7 (quoted in *A Critique of Mau: Mute Compulsion and Other Essays*, p. 41-43).

in his first two drafts of the letter to Vera Zasulich?[102] Or rely on Heinrich on the "merely 'declamatory'" nature of the passage in *Capital* where Marx claims that, "capitalist production begets, with the inexorability of a natural process, its own negation",[103] or overlook Marx' insistence on this very point: that capitalism begets its own negation "with the inexorability of a natural process", referring, in this case too, to that dialectic, *and* to his analysis, in *Capital*, of capitalist production, in his letter to the editorial board of the *Otechestvenniye Zapiski*?[104]

The problem with the denial of Marx' and Engels' determinism and their notion of the dialectic of forces and relations of production as the motive power of historical development and transformations is not that this conception and the determinism based on it are valid theoretical elements: on the contrary they must be regarded as untenable and harmful inasmuch as they hold out the promise that the problems involved in the transition from capitalism to socialism and eventually classless communist society will be solved in and by the very course of historical development – the only difference which may be made by theory and agency being that of shortening and alleviating the birthpangs, or failing to do so. In other words, the problems of class capacities and strategy are in effect minimised or ignored. And by denying, rather than criticising, Marx' and Engels' determinism, the deniers are glossing over this gap.

One may guess that the denial is at bottom caused by the fact that with the failure of Marx' and Engels' expectations and predictions to come true their determinism has become a

---

[102] Marx, ['Entwürfe einer Antwort auf den Brief von V. I. Sassulitsch'], p. 392, p. 397-398.
[103] Marx, *Das Kapital*, 1, p. 791.
[104] Marx, ['Brief an die Redaktion der "Otetschestwennyje Sapiski"'], p. 108-111. Mau, p. 107-108.

liability to Marxian historical materialism, which is therefore misread to the effect that the determinism and expectations were never there, and the predictions were only made for hortatory purposes. Which is not just faulty scholarship, but also a kind of theoretical escapism – as is, of course, the denial of any such failure of Marx' and Engels' expectations and predictions and the insistence that what is taken to be such a failure is only the fact that "the time line for the development of consciousness and agency toward socialist revolution has turned out to be longer than we had thought and hoped for."[105]

It is a cause for concern that several writers have accepted Draper's interpretation of the two sentences opening section I of the *Manifesto*, or themselves interpreted them to the same effect, without wondering about the fact that bourgeois society is not among those mentioned in the two opening sentences or about the contradiction between Draper's reading of them on the one hand and the final pages of the section on the other – let alone the several passages in other Marxian and Engelsian texts where explicit predictions about the inevitable victory of the proletariat and transition from capitalism to socialism and eventually classless communist society are found, including such central texts as the 1859 Preface to *A Contribution to the Critique of Political Economy*, *Capital* (especially ch. 24.7) and *Anti-Dühring*, from the mid-1840s and on. It suggests a general failure to read the textual evidence carefully and with a critical, but open, mind, and, perhaps more likely, the way Marx' and Engels' expectations and predictions about this inevitable transition have, as mentioned above, eventually become a liability:[106] the development from

---

[105] Anonymous reader's report, private communication to this writer from Dr. David Laibman, quoted in Gram-Jensen, *Structure, Agency and Theory*, p. 22.
[106] Cf. the second Essay in Gram-Jensen, *A Revised Historical Materialism*, section c and d for two (Danish) examples of writers

about the beginning of the 20th century, certainly from the failure of socialist parties to live up to their promises at the outbreak of the 1st World War, and on with the Bolshevik revolution in the Zarist Empire, in spite of its incomplete capitalist development, in 1917, the development of the Soviet Union, Stalinism and the trajectory of "real existing socialism" up to and including its demise in the Soviet bloc, and the parallel isolation of class struggle and decline of revolutionary politics in the advanced capitalist societies, looks like an object lesson in the untenability of the idea that the very laws of historical development render the fall of the bourgeoisie and the victory of the working class equally inevitable.

Generally, the unwillingness to recognise the determinism (the belief in the inevitability of the transition from capitalism to socialism and eventually classless communist society) in Marx and Engels, which, in terms of textual evidence, is an unwillingness to see what is demonstrably there, should invite reflection. And so should the unwillingness to recognise the likewise easily demonstrable tension in Marx' and Engels' historical materialism between their conception of historical development as ruled by quasi-natural laws, either because human agents' will, consciousness and intentions are determined by these laws, or because their wills cancel out, leaving it to the laws to rule, on the one hand and their emphasis on human agents as the makers of their own history, albeit on

---

(Sørensen and Thing, respectively) who have changed from accepting that Marx' historical materialism is deterministic to denying (in Sørensen, "Den historiske materialisme i lyset af nyere diskussion om social handlen og social objektivitet", p. 26-27 and Thing, *Hvad Marx og Engels mente med kommunisme?* p. 83) that it is. Further discussion on the subject is found in the second essay in Gram-Jensen: *Experience and Historical Materialism; Structure, Agency and Theory*, Part One, ch.s 2-3 and Appendix Five; the second and seventh essays in *A Critique of Mau: Mute Compulsion and Other Essays* and the second essay in *A Revised Historical Materialism*.

given and inherited conditions and with the traditions of previous generations weighing like a nightmare on their brains, on the other. In both cases, problems in Marx' and Engels' historical materialism – with obvious strategic implications – are denied or ignored instead of being faced and dealt with.

Again, it cannot be both ways: historical development must be understood and accounted for as *either* determined by the said kind of laws *or* in terms of the interaction between social circumstances and agency, and the strategic implications of the answer to this question are unmistakable. If the future will unfold according to implacable laws, the question of revolutionary-socialist strategy is in effect rendered irrelevant insofar as these laws push history towards socialism and eventually communism. If its course depends on the interaction between social circumstances and agency, which seems to be the correct answer, the question of revolutionary-socialist strategy is vitally important.

Marx' and Engels' critique of capitalism as an exploitative, antagonistic, crisis-ridden and alienating mode of production seems correct, and classless communist society defined by the effectively *collective* command of the means, process and outcome of production seems to be the only real alternative. But the question about how to realise it has to be faced and – if possible – solved. The trajectory of "real existing socialism" is a warning that the difficulties are only too real, and have to be overcome.

4. Complementarity.

The preceding argument suggests the *complementarity*[107] between structural and historical analysis: the explanatory logics at these two levels of analysis are different, because human *agency* must be taken into account at the latter in a far stronger sense than at the former, at which agents are abstracted from except as "personifications of economic categories, supports of specific class relations and interests"[108] or "the personifications of the economic relations as the supports of which they confront each other".[109] Structural analysis identifies a specific *logic* imposed by the social structure at the core of which the defining mode and relations of production are found, and the consequent limits to and possibilities of historical development. That is, this analysis identifies the specific limits to the possible, with pressures and probabilities, imposed by the type of society defined by the dominant mode in its turn defined by specific relations of production. What *actually* happens within this field of the possible is the object of *historical* analysis, informed by, but irreducible to, structural analysis. And what makes the difference between structural and historical analysis is – apart from differences of geography, natural resources and climate – precisely *agency*, agents' articulation of their experiences of and responses to their "lived" reality, their *conscious* handling of it according to their experiences of it, which is irreducible to their *mere* role as "personifications of economic categories, supports of specific class relations and interests" or "the personifications of

---

[107] The sense in which "complementarity" is used here is similar to that defined as: "The existence of different aspects of the description of a physical system, seemingly incompatible but both needed for a complete description of the system." (French & Kennedy, p. 370). Cf. Bohr, p. 74.

[108] Marx, *Das Kapital*, 1, p. 16.

[109] Marx, *Das Kapital*, 1, p. 100.

the economic relations as the supports of which they confront each other."

These bearers or supports of economic positions and interests are not the merely passive supports of those positions or of "the guises (*Charaktermasken*) assigned to them by the structure of relations in the social formation."[110] They – we – are thinking beings who articulate their experiences of and responses to their "lived" reality in concrete situations or conjunctures, which include other – economic, political and ideological – issues and conditions, and *according to their horizon of action*,[111] which in its turn involves their experiences and the means at their disposal, and for that matter their individual psychological make-up. They are, in other words, *more than* the mere "personifications of the economic relations as the supports of which they confront each other", and while the abstraction of considering them only as such personifications is legitimate for the purpose of structural analysis, it will not do for those of historical or strategic analysis as this "more" must be expected to influence their mentality, objectives and actions as well as their chances of realising their objectives.[112]

Complementarity has been exemplified by the wave-particle-duality:

> [.....]. A complete description of e. g. an electron or a
> photon cannot be made by observing either wave

---

[110] Althusser & Balibar, p. 320 (Brewster's Glossary, "Support").

[111] Cf. Gram-Jensen, *Structure, Agency and Theory*, p. 1330: "**Horizon of action:** the range of actions appearing possible to agents/actors." To be distinguished from their "**Range of options:** the options objectively available to agents/actors." (p. 1333).

[112] Cf. Levine & Wright and Wright, Levine & Sober, Part I on "Class capacities for struggle – the organizational, ideological and material resources available to class agents" (Wright, Levine & Sober, p. 29).

properties only or only particle properties. Both properties are needed for a complete description, but they are fundamentally impossible to observe simultaneously. The choice of experiment will determine what one is observing.[113]

At the most fundamental level, the specifically human agency – human beings' mental and practical relating to and handling of their "lived" reality, without which there would be no social history in the first place – *cannot*, in any analysis or forecast of historical development, be reduced to the mere serving as bearers or supports of character masks. Again, such reduction is legitimate for the purpose of making a structural analysis of a mode of production which *does* exert a pressure on agents' thought and practice according to their places and functions in the structure which this mode, or the type of society defined by it, constitutes. But it nevertheless amounts to an act of abstraction for analytical purposes, an abstraction from agents as the makers of their own history – under the given and inherited circumstances with which they are directly confronted, and with the tradition of the dead generations weighing like a nightmare on their minds.[114]

We should remember that Marx wrote that,

> The larger the social wealth, the functioning capital, the extent and energy of its growth, hence also the absolute magnitude of the proletariat and the productive power of its labour, the larger the industrial reserve army. The available labour-power is developed for the same reasons as the expansive power of capital.

[113] *Den Store Danske Encyklopædi*, vol. 11, p. 108. Cf. Pais, ch. 14. e, and p. 446.
[114] Cf. Marx, *The Eighteenth Brumaire of Louis Bonaparte*, p. 146 (*MEW*, 8, p. 115).

Therefore, the relative magnitude of the industrial reserve army grows with the potentials of wealth. But the larger this reserve army relative to the active army of labourers, the more massive the consolidated overpopulation the misery of which stands in an inverse ratio to the pains of their work. The larger finally the ragamuffin stratum of the working class and the industrial reserve army, the larger the official pauperism. *This is the absolute, general law of capitalist accumulation.* Like all other laws it is modified in its eventuation by manifold circumstances the analysis of which does not belong here.[115]

And, in the third volume of *Capital*, that,

The specific economic form in which unpaid surplus labour is pumped from the immediate producers determines the relationship between master and servant as it springs immediately from production itself and in its turn reacts on it as a determinant [*und seinerseits bestimmend auf sie zurückwirkt*]. But on this the whole formation of the economic community [*Gemeinwesen*] which springs from the relations of production themselves, and thus at the same time its specific political form, is based. It is every time the immediate relationship of the owners of the means of production [*Produktionsbedingungen*] to the immediate producers – a relationship the current form of which always quite naturally corresponds to a specific stage of development of the mode of labour and thus its social power of production – in which we find the innermost secret, the hidden basis of the whole social construction and hence also the political form of the relations of sover-

---

[115] Marx, *Das Kapital*, 1, p. 673-674. According to Witt-Hansen (p. 115) "absolute" is in the Hegelian sense: "abstract".

eignty and dependence, in brief the current specific form of the state. This does not mean that the same economic basis – the same in terms of the main conditions – cannot, due to countless different empirical circumstances, natural conditions, race relations, external historical influences etcetera, exhibit endless variations and shades which can only be understood by analysing these empirically given circumstances.[116]

We cannot introduce the concrete circumstances "the analysis of which does not belong here" into the structural analysis, because then it is no more a (rigorous) structural analysis, as the developmental logic inherent in the pure structure is interacting with, and hence interfered with by, historical circumstances, including the interventions into its course of development by human actors.

In the historical analysis, on the other hand, it is precisely the *actual* interaction between social circumstances, *whether these are of structural or historical provenance*, on the one hand and agency on the other which is the object of investigation – and the developmental logic in its pure, undisturbed unfolding (which is *only* found in structural analysis, that is, by means of abstraction, *not* in actual history which always eventuates in a specific place at a specific point in time and in specific concrete circumstances) cannot explain that interaction exhaustively. The historical analysis must be informed by the knowledge acquired from the structural analysis which in its turn must involve that acquired from the analysis of historical development as the mode of production is never found in its "ideal average" in the real world. We can afford to ignore

---

[116] Marx, *Das Kapital*, 3, p. 799-800; cf. p. 839 on the "ideal average" of the capitalist mode of production as distinct from "the real movement of competition".

neither structurally *nor* historically determined social circumstances.

It is impossible to understand the development of capitalist societies without reference to the developmental logic which is peculiar to the capitalist mode of production with its specific mechanism of exploitation and exchange,[117] the peculiar nature of which is at the bottom of the drive for technological development (which proved less effective in "real existing socialism"[118]), the possibility and limits of bourgeois democracy, and the conditions for the isolation of class struggle. But it is also impossible to *derive* their concrete, and different, developments from the analysis of capitalism "on its ideal average" as, again, "the structure" or "ideal average" in its pure form does not *exist* in a material sense, but only as abstractions from real, more or less deviant, social formations of different types.

At this point it is relevant to consider the intellectual feat accomplished by Marx and Engels. To arrive at an understanding of capitalism as a mode of production and a type of society defined by a specific mechanism of exploitation different from that of other types of class societies required a major effort of abstraction and *structural* analysis. Few who take the trouble of reading the *Grundrisse* will probably fail to be impressed by the way Marx dissects the theories of political economists and then returns to them again for a second and

---

[117] Cf. Marx, *Das Kapital*, 3, p. 799-800 quoted above, where the distance between structural and historical analysis is noted. Anderson, *Lineages of the Absolutist State*, p. 403: "Capitalism is the first mode of production in history in which the means whereby the surplus is pumped out of the direct producer is 'purely' economic in form – the wage contract: the equal exchange between free agents which reproduces, hourly and daily, inequality and oppression." And Therborn, "The Rule of Capital and the Rise of Democracy".
[118] Nove, p. 82 and passim.

third analysis. To arrive at the conception of the (pre)history of human society as a process of development and transitions from one mode of production and type of society to another, thus avoiding the reduction of the handling of social problems to the introduction of various reforms, pointing, instead, to *classless* society as the only real means of overcoming exploitation, oppression, inequality and social antagonisms – this too required abstraction and structural analysis, which in its turn had to draw on the study of history, that is *historical* analysis, in order to be based on knowledge rather than speculation.

One of the characteristics of the capitalist mode of production and type of society is its unique drive for technological development promising to make it possible to eliminate the danger of "all the old shit" of class societies returning because of general want, with the consequent struggles over necessities:[119] the same drive for technological development which may have made Marx and Engels read the dialectic of forces and relations of production back into the past as the motive power of historical development and transformations.

As we can see from the passages quoted or cited, Marx did indeed acknowledge the difference between structural and historical analysis, the difference between the capitalist mode of production "on its ideal average" and the social circumstances in the countries dominated by this mode,[120] but did not, alas, draw the conclusion from this that reliable *historical* predictions cannot be based *merely* on the *structural* analysis of the mode and the type of society. The reason for this failure on his part is, again, probably that the idea of history as a

---

[119] Marx & Engels, *Die deutsche Ideologie*, p. 34-35.
[120] Cf. Engels, "Engels an Conrad Schmidt in Zürich 12. März 1895", p. 431-433 on the distance between concepts and reality (and Thompson, *The Poverty of Theory and Other Essays*, p. 50 ff.).

process determined by *laws* of development comparable to those ruling natural processes came so naturally to 19th-century people in advanced societies.

Marx' words, quoted above, on the "endless variations and gradations due to countless different empirical circumstances" suggest what is meant by the complementarity between structural and historical analysis. This observation seems simply to imply that explaining these endless variations requires analysing the empirically given circumstances giving rise to them *in their own right* rather than *deriving* them from the analysis of capital "on its ideal average". The irreducibility of historical analysis to such derivation[121] is also suggested by the assumption that, "The supports of the character masks of capital are under the mute compulsion of capitalism to accumulate capital, but they have to find out *how*, in specific structurally and historically determined conditions and without any guarantee that the line of action they choose is optimal, or even realistic."[122]

The point should be obvious: even if we accept the idea that capitalist actors are to a considerable degree reduced to supports of their position as such – at least insofar as they want to hold on to this position – they cannot be taken to be omni- or prescient, nor can they escape their "lived" reality up to the relevant moment, with its specific course, experiences and effects on their intellectual and psychological make-up, or whatever mental characteristics they may otherwise have. And the current situation in which they have to make

---

[121] Here the term "derivation" denotes the deduction of explanations or concepts directly from structural analysis, e. g. the explanation of functions or actions on the part of the capitalist state by reference to the functionality of this type of state to capitalist accumulation.

[122] Gram-Jensen, *A Critique of Mau:* Mute Compulsion *and Other Essays*, p. 150.

82

decisions is always and irreducibly *historical*, within the limits to the possible imposed by the dominant mode of production and its "ideal average". Which is also suggested by Engels' remark that concepts never correspond completely to the reality from which they are abstracted.[123]

We cannot explain (or foresee!) the outcome of the interaction between agency and capitalism/capitalist relations of production (economy) if we do not understand the capitalist mode of production – that is, without being informed by the structural analysis of it; but, on the other hand, capitalism does not, in actual history, develop and have effects in the abstract: it will develop and have effects in a concrete process of interaction between itself and human actions, in conjunctures which themselves eventuate from the same process (basically that of historical development) which, through the interaction between mode of production and agency (and all other relevant circumstances), delimits the field of the possible, with its pressures and probabilities at any given moment in time and place. Hence the historical development of capitalism and capitalist social formations cannot be derived from the (structural) analysis of the capitalist mode of production: it is, and will be, irreducible to the efficacy of the regularities of the mode identifiable by means of the structural analysis of it. Which is, again, down to the fact that the development of capitalist society cannot be understood if abstracting from agency, that is, the actual ways in which agents articulate their various experiences of and responses to their "lived" reality – which is itself the product of historical development up to the point in time concerned.

So, again, Marx and Engels actually warned against failing to recognise the distance between structural and historical

---

[123] Engels, "Engels an Conrad Schmidt, 12. März 1895", p. 431-433.

analysis of capitalism; but all the same, in spite of the irreducibility of historical analysis to structural analysis or what is derivable from the latter, they assumed that the transition from capitalism to socialism and eventually classless communist society is inevitable: inevitable because of the dialectic of forces and relations of production they supposed to be the motive power of historical development and transformations. Thus, according to their assumptions, the irreducibility of the factors making actual historical developments deviate from those derivable from structural analysis does *not* overrule the dialectic of forces and relations of production, nor does the irreducibility of human agency. And thus, the tension in Marx' and Engels' historical materialism remains. All the historical deviations notwithstanding, the laws supposed to rule the development of society and the transitions from one type of society to another, determining the will, consciousness and intentions of agents,[124] are assumed to guarantee that the prehistory of human society will close with capitalism.[125]

Structural analysis includes more or less strong *tendencies* inherent in the dominant mode defining the type of society (e. g. the pressure to accumulate capital tending to result in larger capitals, concentration of capital, oligopolies, political power of owners of large capitals etcetera); historical analysis includes all the specific traits of the given social formation, and actual events affecting its development, whether dependent on the dominant mode of the society or not.

The isolation of class struggle is accountable for in its capitalist context, but hardly derivable from the structural analysis of either capital(ism) or the given social formation, depending

---

[124] Marx, *Das Kapital*, 1, p. 25-27.
[125] Marx, *A Contribution to the Critique of Political Economy*, p. 22 (*MEW*, 13, p. 9).

as it does on political decisions and actions in specific historical conjunctures.

Historical development involves agency, and for that reason it is irreducible to consequences of causes reducible to structurally given factors, and hence historical analysis is irreducible to structural analysis, although the structure of the mode of production sets limits to the possible with pressures and probabilities. The active, creative aspect of agency, agents' conscious relating to their "lived" reality, their articulation of their experiences of and responses to this "lived" reality, is irreducible to the dynamic inherent in the structure of the dominant mode (which will interact with other modes, either within the social formation(s) in question or through its or their interaction with other social formations). One aspect of this is the irreducibility of agents to the mere bearers or supports of character masks imposed on them by the structure of the dominant mode of production or by the type of society in question.

Obviously, the formation of working-class agents' ideology, whether revolutionary-socialist, gradualist, reformist, liberal, conservative or whatever, cannot be understood in isolation from its concrete, historical context: standards of living, relations of power, economic conjunctures, levels of employment and unemployment, current policies and historical experiences, media – but it does influence the choices and behaviour of agents, the class capacity of the working class and hence the course of history, making the isolation of class struggle more or less likely.

Indeed, *ideally* one of the tasks of historical analysis must be to explain what prompted and shaped agents' actual articulation of their experiences of and responses to their "lived" reality, that is, what they thought about this reality and how they reacted on it, *and* what effects this had on the course of historical development.

It should, hopefully, be obvious that this is not to suggest that human ideas are the unmoved mover of historical development, unconditioned by, and the sole condition of, social circumstances. The point is that social circumstances do not trigger, change and shape historical social development except as conditioning human agency and through human agency, that is, human actors' *handling* of their "lived" reality according to what they think about it. Historical development is a process of interaction between social circumstances and agency, both being reproduced *and* changed in the course of it. There would be no such thing as social history, only biological development, if human actors could not and did not *respond to* and *handle* their social circumstances, that "lived" reality of human actors which includes all circumstances affecting them.

To fulfil the ideal task of historical analysis mentioned above by accounting for human agents' actual responses to their social circumstances, that is, to explain why they articulate precisely the experiences of these circumstances which they actually do, and according to which they try to handle their "lived" reality, may well prove impossible. The precise relation of cause (social circumstances) and effects (experiences and responses in their *precise* articulation) will most likely be hard to establish. If we accept the conception of structural determination in the last instance as the delimitation of a field of the possible, with pressures and probabilities,[126] the establishment of a direct relation of identifiable cause and specific effect must be taken to require the charting of the actual process by which the former leads to the latter (the more or less *probable*, but not *derivable* effect of the former, which may well

---

[126] Wright, *Class, Crisis and the State*, p. 15-16.

in its turn involve a *complex* of social circumstances and developments). But a relation between the actual social developments and changes in terms of experiences and responses may be established and at least to some extent related to agents' social positions and interests, while also taking the fact of ideological *struggles* into account. Anderson,[127] Nove[128] and Levine & Wright suggest the different conditions of class struggle, and social practice generally, in different types of society. And Esping-Andersen, Goodin et al. and Wilkinson & Pickett demonstrate that the development of different (advanced) capitalist societies and over time – with considerable effects on agents' "lived" reality – cannot be explained by or derived from the analysis of capitalism or the capitalist type of society "on its ideal average".

Again, agents' minds do not automatically *reflect* their positions and functions in the structure of a mode of production and a given social formation:[129] they will have to *find out* who they are, what their situation is, and what can and should be done about it – which is easier or more difficult according to their respective positions[130] and the various conjunctures. Hence, in *historical* analysis this distinction between (bearers/supports of) character masks on the one hand and actual agency on the other must be taken into account, as noted in the essay "Human Agency" in *A Critique of Mau:* Mute

---

[127] Anderson, *Lineages of the Absolutist State*, p. 403-404.

[128] Nove, p. 82, p. 101.

[129] In fact, the passage from structural to historical analysis starts with the analysis of a type of society, which is more than the mode of production defining it, continuing to that of a specific social formation, which will exhibit specific traits within the given type of society, and interact with other formations, and on to the analysis of one or more formations in a given conjuncture.

[130] It is easy for owners of capital to see that their income and position depend on this ownership, whereas the capitalist mechanism of exploitation may remain opaque to workers and capitalists alike.

Compulsion *and Other Essays*: even the bearers or supports of the capitalist character mask, whether owners or salaried managers, who know that their mission is to make capital profitable, to accumulate, have to find out *how* in order to do so, and may fail to succeed.[131]

Human beings inhabit a material world in which many processes are indeed ruled by natural laws in the literal sense of the term, but while human beings have to *find out* about such laws in order to handle them effectively according to their own ends, they are able to relate *consciously*, and in different ways, to their environment, that is, their "lived" reality, the totality of factors affecting them, including, within certain limits and on irreducible conditions, by handling it and changing it materially – whether their specific *social* reality or the world in general is concerned.

Agents' articulation of their experiences of and responses to their "lived" reality at any given point in time and space, and changes in it, may *itself* be (more or less approximately and exhaustively) accounted for as the outcome of various identifiable aspects of other developments in that reality itself, and/or adduced as the cause(s) of such developments, that is, considered as part of the actual process of historical development, interacting with and causing changes in social circumstances. In the former case, the emphasis is on the process of articulation and the causes of its actual course, in the latter on its outcome and its effect on historical development. In both cases, explanations after the event will be more realistic than predictions.

To be sure, the given circumstances will delimit a field of the possible – with pressures and probabilities – within which

---

[131] Gram-Jensen, *A Critique of Mau: Mute Compulsion and Other Essays*, p. 150. Cf. Robinson, p. 94-95.

agents' experiences and responses are articulated and have their effects. We are, of course, able to make some general predictions, such as the one that support for a political line causing a major economic recession (whether related to economic sabotage or not) is likely to decline,[132] although most often of the "other things equal" kind. But uncertainty regarding the factors and circumstances involved, and the sheer complexity of their interaction, will limit the precision of predictions, especially, of course, regarding the long run.[133] And again, new solutions may be found (and may turn out to be more or less successful or the opposite), and new strategies and/or tactics adopted, with results that were unforeseeable in advance.

So far it has not been possible to predict outcomes precisely, and hence, even apart from rivalling attempts to influence the process, for actors to consistently shape it according to their wishes by adapting their own actions and communication accordingly. For practical purposes, at least, the number of possible outcomes in given circumstances – the number and effects of which must in any case be considered impossible to identify precisely – must be taken to be more than one. Which may in its turn be considered related to human beings' very ability to relate consciously to their "lived" reality: if their consciousness and their articulation of experiences and responses to this reality did not involve a degree of open-endedness, including the articulation of intrinsically new ideas, the historical, social development of human society in all its

---

[132] Cf. Gram-Jensen, *Structure, Agency and Theory*, Part Three, ch. 7.c.
[133] Some short-run responses may, if the actors, factors and general circumstances involved are well known, be predicted with reasonable confidence, but even slight differences in the effects eventuating from the interaction between social circumstances and agency will be likely to cause variations making the further development uncertain.

various aspects and forms had hardly been possible in the first place.

One consequence of this is the impossibility of foreseeing future historical development due to the fact that *"we cannot anticipate today what we shall know only tomorrow"*[134] – or what we rightly or wrongly believe tomorrow. The future development in terms of technology and knowledge and its effects on social circumstances, and thus the "lived" reality of agents, and hence agents' future articulations of their experiences of and responses to that "lived" reality, cannot be anticipated with precision – and hence the same goes for historical development as a whole. The interaction between social circumstances and agency – and hence the process of historical development – are open-ended in the dual sense of being impossible to foresee with precision or certainty, and being irreducible to effects of knowable laws of development.[135] This has significance for the question of the definition of social classes, which illustrates the complementarity between structural and historical analysis.

---

[134] Popper, *The Poverty of Historicism*, p. vii.
[135] Cf. Gram-Jensen, *Experience and Historical Materialism*, section d. of the third essay on the question, and the dubiousness, of strict determinism.

5. The Definition of Classes.

In *Classes*, Erik Olin Wright specified "the general theoretical constraints that the requisite concepts must respect" in the endeavour to define social classes. These constraints were:

1. *Class structure imposes limits on class formation, class consciousness and class struggle.*
2. *Class structures constitute the essential qualitative lines of social demarcation in the historical trajectories of social change.*
3. *The concept of class is a relational concept.*
4. *The social relations which define classes are intrinsically antagonistic rather than symmetrical.*
5. *The objective basis of these antagonistic interests is exploitation.*
6. *The fundamental basis of exploitation is to be found in the social relations of production.*[136]

Wright concedes that "a simple wage-labour criterion for the working class" conforms to five of these six constraints, but argues that,

> [.....]. Where this view of the 'middle class' fails dismally is in satisfying the first theoretical constraint. It is hard to see how a definition of the working class as all wage-earners could provide a satisfactory structural basis for explaining class formation, class consciousness and class struggle. It is certainly not the case that 'all things being equal' top managers are generally more likely to side with industrial workers than with the bourgeoisie in class struggles. Indeed, it is difficult to imagine any conceivable circumstances when this would be the case. Drawing the boundary criteria for the working class at wage-earners, therefore, does not

---

[136] Wright, p. 26-37.

create a category which is in any meaningful sense homogeneous with respect to its effects.[137]

This argument in Wright has been criticised by this writer in *A Critique of Mau:* Mute Compulsion *and Other Essays.*[138] The question which is emphasised in the present text is: why is it precisely Wright's first constraint which a definition of the working class as all wage-earners does not conform to? And the answer is very simple, and very enlightening on the problem of the interaction between social circumstances and agency, and the problem of this interaction and of agency in historical materialism: because this is the one constraint which concerns agents' *consciousness*, and thus their articulation of their experiences of and responses to their "lived" reality, and therefore also the conditions imposed on this process of articulation by their "lived" reality. It is demonstrable *why* these conditions – as well as the nature of the process itself[139] – do not guarantee a uniform working-class consciousness, let alone a revolutionary-socialist one, in a working class which, in capitalist relations of production, is defined by wage-labour, or more precisely as agents who, as non-owners of (other) means of production (than their labour-power) have to put their labour-power up for sale and are thus (potential) objects of exploitation in the form of unpaid labour extorted as surplus value or surplus labour.[140]

---

137 Wright, p. 38-39.

138 Gram-Jensen, *A Critique of Mau:* Mute Compulsion *& Other Essays*, p. 140-146.

139 A process including attempts to pre-empt or counter the development and spread of a revolutionary (or for that matter reformist) consciousness, which in its turn points towards the structurally and historically determined distribution of such resources as are relevant in that context.

140 Cf. Gram-Jensen, *Structure, Agency and Theory*, p. 1335.

Human agents relate consciously to their own existence – but this does not mean that their consciousness is necessarily correct or uniform, not even insofar as they belong to the same class. And therefore classes and their boundaries cannot be defined in terms of consciousness, least *perhaps* the capitalist working class, given the special, opaque nature of capitalist exploitation, the different conditions of work and pay of members of the class as defined here and the conditions tending towards reformism, gradualism, competition between various categories of workers (along divisions of trade, gender, ethnicity, nationality, religion, or whatever – competition over the access to jobs, wages and status). Be it as it may with the capitalist working class compared to other contemporary or historical classes, human agents' articulation of their experiences of and responses to their (actual, concrete, historically as well as structurally determined) "lived" reality cannot be expected to be precisely predictable, or to produce only one variety of consciousness.

It must, though, be expected that it is easier for members of the capitalist class to realise what their fundamental class interest is: maintaining their capitals and therefore also capitalist relations of production and capitalist society as well as conditions enabling (and preferably as favourable as possible to) the continued accumulation of capital, i. e. the appropriation of surplus value and surplus labour (though owners and managers of capital may not be conscious of this exploitation). As for top managers who occupy the position of sellers of their labour-power, the owners of capital would presumably very much prefer to employ them on conditions of work and pay comparable to that of less privileged workers, if they could nevertheless be trusted to perform their functions adequately. As this is unlikely, they come to work and live on conditions comparable to those of owners of capital, much like select slaves atypically occupying positions of great power and great privileges in earlier societies.

This approach to the definition and analysis of classes is based on and expressed in a number of conceptual definitions which are put forward in the Glossary to *Structure, Agency and Theory*:[141]

> **Exploitation**: the basic pattern of exploitation and consequently the class division inherent in an exploitative mode of production are determined by the relations of production defining that mode: a social surplus product is appropriated by a category (class) of agents who did not produce it, rather than by that category (class) of agents who did by virtue of the combination of agents' relations to the means of production and each other defining the relations of production, and agents' differentiated positions in that combination.

> **Relations of production**: the combination of relations to the means of production and each other into which agents enter in their social existence, and by which a specific pattern of disposal of the means of production and the social product is established.

> **Mode of Production**: defined by the specific relations of production. A mode of production is dominant insofar as it determines the structure of the society in which it coexists with other modes which are subordinated to the structure determined by the dominant one.

> **Type of Society**: a category of social formations (feudal, capitalist, socialist etcetera) defined – because of structural determination – by the mode of production

---

[141] Gram-Jensen, *Structure, Agency and Theory*, p. 1327-1335.

that is dominant within them, and with a corresponding type of state.

Capitalist exploitation: the extortion and appropriation of surplus value or surplus labour via the buying and selling of labour[142] as a commodity which is put to use by the buyer, thus relying on market mechanisms rather than involving extra-economic means of exploitation contrary to e.g. those involved in feudal or slave exploitation.

Capitalist Class: the exploiting class in capitalist relations of production, defined by ownership of means of production in the form of capital which allows the class to appropriate surplus value or surplus labour. Positions in the class, bourgeois class positions, are defined as those of agents whose chief source of income is ownership of capital.

Working class: the working class in capitalist relations of production is defined as a class of non-owners of means of production who consequently have to sell their labour-power and are thus (potential) objects of exploitation in the form of unpaid labour extorted as surplus value or surplus labour. Working-class positions are defined as those of agents whose chief source of income is the selling of their labour-power.

Petty Bourgeoisie: this class is defined as depending on simple commodity production, consisting of agents employing their own labour-power on their own

---

[142] This definition, which is the one used in *Structure, Agency and Theory*, p. 1327, is not quite correct: as stated on p. 1335, as part of the definition of the working class, it is the sale of *labour-power* which allows the capitalist exploitation to take place.

means of production, in the non-collective manufacturing or circulation of commodities, this mode of production in itself implying no relation of exploitation (although empirically the exploitation of employed labour is found in such manufacturing and circulation). Petty-bourgeois positions are defined as those of agents whose chief income is their own labour (possibly as a family) with their own means of production.

Interests: in the present text a distinction is made between a. *class interests*, or *structural interests* defined at the level of the mode of production and b. *historical interests* definable at the level of actual history, whether identical with class interests or not. Historical interests may in their turn be regarded as either *fundamental*, i.e. concerning the maintenance or abolition (or dominance or subordination) of modes of production, or *immediate*, i.e. concerning issues within the framework of a given mode or type of society.

Objective interests: the realisation or maintenance of a state of "lived" reality directly or indirectly making it more likely that agents experience (a higher degree of) gratification or avoid experiencing the opposite is in their objective interest – whether experienced as such or not.

And consequently, the following approach to the definition of classes is chosen as the most realistic and consistent:

Class: in the present text classes are defined at the level of abstraction of the mode of production, delimited in their antagonistic relationship to each other by the fundamental interests in the maintenance or abolition of the mode and the corresponding type of society implied by positions as exploiters and exploited in the relations of exploitation defining the mode.[143]

The argument may seem complicated, but the suggested approach seems to be the only one allowing a logically consistent drawing of the boundaries between classes and defining them theoretically, if "class" is to be understood in terms of relations of exploitation and conflicting interests. And in any case, if agents' consciousness is *historically* determined and *variable* on the basis of constant positions in the relations of production and within the limits to the possible drawn by these relations, as well as relative to agents' objective interests, this consciousness is not a useful criterion of class – regardless of its very real and obvious *strategic* importance.

Thus, against Thompson's statements that, "I do not see class as a 'structure', nor even as a 'category', but as something which in fact happens (and can be shown to have happened) in human relationships" and that, "[.....] class happens when some men, as a result of common experiences (inherited or shared), feel and articulate the identity of their interests as between themselves, and as against other men whose interests are different from (and usually opposed to) theirs",[144] it is necessary to distinguish between *the consciousness of classes* in the sense of the (forms of) consciousness actually found in the members of a class on the one hand and *class consciousness* in the sense of the consciousness of belonging to a certain class (in contradistinction from other classes), with the consequent answers to the question, "who are we, what is our situation and what can and should be done about it?" on the other.

Even if the class positions in the capitalist mode of production remain definable in the suggested way and are of a

[143] Gram-Jensen, *Structure, Agency and Theory*, p. 1327.
[144] Thompson, *The Making of the English Working Class*, p. 9-10.

constant nature, the "lived" reality of agents, and hence the conditions on which they articulate their experiences of and responses to this "lived" reality, are constantly changing as part of a historical development of which human actors are themselves the active makers, under, and interacting with, objective conditions.

One obvious cause of the (potential and real) lack of a direct reflection of positions in the relations of production in agents' consciousness – quite apart, in capitalism, from the opaqueness of the mechanism of its basic pattern of exploitation[145] – is the complex flow of situations, conflicts and changing conditions to which agents are exposed, and which are irreducible to a simple conflict between class interests, though interacting with class divisions and (conflicts over) class interests: conflicts over fractional interests and divisions in terms of gender, "race", ethnicity, religion etcetera, over divisions in terms of power and for and against more or less democratic or authoritarian political forms of government, conflicts between social formations – with the more or less constant choice between fighting for class, sectional or individual interests. Agents may, in other words, articulate different answers to the question, "who are we, what is our situation and what can and should be done about?", according to their different positions not just in class but also in a number of other hierarchies and groups, and to their estimation of their situation and chances.

---

[145] Agents whose chief source of income is the sale of their labour-power may, because of the manifold positions, functions and conditions experienced at workplaces, as well as all the differences of education, lifestyles (habitus) and status, not consider themselves members of the working class, or, given the lack of differences between the politico-legal status of classes in capitalism, for that matter of *any* specific *class*.

Thus, rather than looking for more or less uniform forms of *consciousness*, we should look for uniform *interests* in terms of the maintenance or abolition of given relations of production, and alternatives to those relations derivable from agents' positions in those relations. And when doing so, some – rather trivial – assumptions about human beings' physical and psychological needs (in order to stay alive and to be more or less satisfied with their life) must (and can) be made.[146]

This will also help us focus on the crucial question of the relationship between interests and consciousness – and between *fundamental* (class) interests on the one hand and *immediate* (class, fractional/sectional or individual) interests on the other – and between the ranges of options and the horizons of action of agents/actors. This, in its turn, points towards two major themes in *Structure, Agency and Theory*, and of the suggested revision of historical materialism: agents' articulation of their experiences of and responses to their "lived" reality, and the *effect of isolation* or *isolation of class struggle*: the limitation of social practice (i. e. of agents' responses to their "lived" reality) to such forms as do not objectively threaten to disrupt the type of society and the dominant relations of production,[147] as a historical phenomenon in advanced capitalist societies. Both of which may contribute to a more realistic idea of the interaction between social circumstances and agency as a historical process, and of the problems facing revolutionary-socialist politics.

Engels' idea that the tug of war between various intentions and consequent actions adds up to parallelograms of forces in the last resort allowing history to develop "in the manner of a natural process" and "essentially subject to the same laws

---

[146] As Wright does in *Classes*, p. 28, p. 36.
[147] Gram-Jensen, *Structure, Agency and Theory*, p. 1329; cf. Part Three, ch. 1.

of motion",[148] is dealt with above and in *A Revised Historical Materialism* and does not need to be discussed in much further detail here, apart from noting that if it is assumed to be valid, the success or failure of the working class to organise around its fundamental class interest in the transition from capitalism to socialism and eventually classless communist society, and to elaborate and apply an effective strategy to accomplish it, is by implication irrelevant. Indeed, the idea implies the inability of human agency to make any real difference at all to the course of history.

The alternative argued in *A Revised Historical Materialism* as well as *Experience and Historical Materialism* and *Structure, Agency and Theory* is, firstly, the substitution of the conception of the dialectic of forces and relations of production as the motive power of historical development and transformations by that of *the interaction between social circumstances and agency* as this motive power; and, secondly, the conception of the interaction between social circumstances and agency in terms of *structural determination* or *determination in the last instance* rather than Engels' parallelograms, structural determination or determination in the last instance meaning "[.....] a pattern of causation setting limits to the possible, with the exclusion of some forms and a range of probability of others, from the all but impossible to the inevitable. The number of possible outcomes within the field of the possible thus delimited is finite, but rarely no more than one. The structure of a type of society, in particular, sets limits to the possible within which historical circumstances determine actual eventuation."[149] This conception, in its turn, suggests the *open-endedness* of the process of historical development, not in the sense that anything

---

[148] Engels, "Engels an Joseph Bloch in Königsberg, 21./22. September 1890", p. 464.
[149] Gram-Jensen, *Structure, Agency and Theory*, p. 1328. Cf. Wright, *Class, Crisis and the State*, p. 15-17.

goes, but in the sense that human agency, agents' specific articulation of their experiences of and responses to their "lived" reality, may make a real difference to the course of historical development, including, in certain historical circumstances, the difference between the maintenance or the transformation of the given type of society.

It should be obvious that one cannot speak of human history, the history of human societies, their development and transitions from one type of society to another except in terms of human *agency*. No such process of social – as distinct from biological – development is conceivable without agents *responding* to their "lived" reality, and thus without their articulation of their experiences of and responses to this "lived" reality: that is, their conscious, practical relationship to their social existence, their active *handling*, in consciousness and materially, of their "lived" reality, the *interaction* between social circumstances and agency.

Obviously, this interaction thus involves agents' consciousness, will and intentions interacting with those of other agents, and the conditions for this interaction and for its actual effects. And it should be obvious, too, that one cannot expect agents' wills to *cancel out*, thus leaving any causal efficacy to laws of historical development independent of, or determining, agents' will, consciousness and intentions, inexorably pushing historical development towards a foreseeable terminus or *telos*. Because of human agents' consciousness, their conscious, and practical, active, formative relationship with their (social) existence, historical development is a process *sui generis*, causally irreducible to anything determined by laws comparable to those of natural processes. Just as the interaction of wills/intentions A, B and C must be taken to be different from that between wills/intentions D, E and F: *what* agents want must be assumed to make a difference in terms of the outcome of the interaction between their wills, including the interaction between their different *actions*, which cannot be isolated from their will, consciousness, and intentions, as these emerge from the process of agents' articulation of their experiences of and responses to their "lived" reality. A process which is an intrinsic, irreducible part of historical development. All of which means that human beings make their own history, "under the given and inherited circumstances with which they are directly confronted."[150] This in its turn means that agents respond to their given conditions, to the conflicts between responses and to the process of development determined by the interaction between the given – but not static – social circumstances and the changes taking place in them on the one hand, and agency on the other.

It also seems obvious that if the forces entering into the parallelogram of forces are not equally strong, their relative strength will influence the actual outcome – which is visible from the different developments in capitalist (and other) societies, e. g. those of "The Three Worlds of Welfare Capitalism" in advanced capitalism.[151] In other words, in the interaction between social circumstances and agency the class capacities of different classes, and the way actors use them or fail to use them, the strategies chosen and the extent to which agents are (effectively) organised around them (which is of course in its turn also determined by the objective conditions on which agents act), will make a difference.

The strategic implications of capitalism, the identification of its mechanism of exploitation with its implications in terms of class divisions and the nature of class interests (how is capitalist exploitation to be eliminated? Who make up the potentially revolutionary class? How is it (or which parts of it) to

---

[150] Marx, *The Eighteenth Brumaire of Louis Bonaparte*, p. 146 (*MEW*, 8, p. 115).
[151] Esping-Andersen.

be mobilised for a revolutionary transition, and how is that transition to be accomplished? What are the structurally given hindrances, and how can they be overcome?) required a structural analysis of the mode (and the type of social formation). To *accomplish* the organisation of the capitalist working class around its fundamental class interest in accomplishing the transition from capitalism to socialism and eventually classless communist society requires historical (including conjunctural) analysis as well in order to establish what is to be done, and can be done, in the current situation.

Objective Interests.

As for the argument on the conception of "objective interests", this term is, as mentioned above, defined as follows in *Structure, Agency and Theory*: "the realisation or maintenance of a state of "lived" reality directly or indirectly making it more likely that agents experience (a higher degree of) gratification or avoid experiencing the opposite is in their objective interest – whether experienced as such or not."[152] It is, in other words, expressly stated that "objective" does *not* mean "(necessarily) actually experienced by agents *as* their interests", but refers to the assumption that their realisation will make it more likely that agents experience (a higher degree of) gratification or avoid the opposite; that, in other words, their realisation corresponds to the fulfilment of some needs of agents, such as material welfare (agents being able to consume more and/or toil less) and their capacity to act (make effective choices about their situation/life – that is, not only choose within a minimum of limits, but also act effectively on their choices).[153] An objective working-class interest in the transition from capitalism to socialism and eventually classless communist society follows from the assumption of those interests as objective interests, but this does not imply that

---

[152] Gram-Jensen, *Structure, Agency and Theory*, p. 1331.
[153] Cf. Wright, *Classes*, p. 36, p. 28.

working-class agents will inevitably articulate or come to articulate them as such interests, let alone act in them. As observed in *Experience and Historical Materialism, Structure, Agency and Theory* and *A Revised Historical Materialism*, "there is no guarantee that agents will necessarily *act on* their objective interests – or that they *never* will."[154]

It would be absurd to argue that agents' articulation of their experiences and responses is not influenced by what is there to be experienced and responded to, that is, their "lived" reality. The very survival of and historical development of the human species would be impossible if there were no such relation. But judging from historical evidence it would be equally absurd to argue that this "lived" reality can only be experienced and responded to in *one* way by agents, or agents belonging to the same class (in the sense of "class" defined here).

In the 1859 Preface to *A Contribution to the Critique of Political Economy*, Marx states, at the very start of the summary of "The general conclusion at which I arrived and which, once reached, became the guiding principle of my studies",[155] the following well-known sentences:

> [.....]. In the social production of their existence, men inevitably enter into definite relations, which are independent of their will, namely relations of production appropriate to a given stage in the development of their material forces of production. The totality of these relations of production constitutes the economic structure of society, the real foundation, on which

---

[154] Gram-Jensen, *Experience and Historical Materialism*, p. 144; *Structure, Agency and Theory*, p. 282; *A Revised Historical Materialism*, p. 77; cf. *A Critique of Mau: Mute Compulsion and Other Essays*, p. 143.
[155] Marx, *A Contribution to the Critique of Political Economy*, p. 20 (*MEW*, 13, p. 8).

arises a legal and political superstructure and to which correspond definite forms of social consciousness. The mode of production of material life conditions the general process of social, political and intellectual life [*Die Produktionsweise des materiellen Lebens bedingt den sozialen, politischen und geistigen Lebensprozeß überhaupt*]. It is not the consciousness of men that determines their existence, but their social existence that determines their consciousness.[156]

The implications of this depend on the way "determines [*bedingt*]" is understood. If it is understood in a reductive sense, denoting the one-to-one reflection of the causation by the mode of material life in the consciousness of agents and thus their social, political and intellectual life, then the latter is, according to Marx, derivable form the former. And then human consciousness is the derivable and simple outcome and reflection of the mode of production of material life. If so, Marx' conception of this relationship suffers from the weakness of such strict determinist conceptions of it: it reduces the formation of human consciousness to a process strictly parallel to those making us sweat or causing rain, and then the question whether our thoughts are true of false would be unanswerable and thus meaningless. And this would be true of Marx' thinking in general and historical materialism generally too.[157] Marx does, however, also state in the next sentences in the1859 Preface that,

> [.....]. At a certain stage of development, the material productive forces of society come into conflict with the existing relations of production or – this merely expresses the same thing in legal terms – with the

---

[156] Marx, *A Contribution to the Critique of Political Economy*, p. 20-21 (*MEW*, 13, p. 8-9).
[157] Favrholdt, p. 159, p. 281-283.

property relations within the framework of which they have operated hitherto. From forms of development of the productive forces these relations turn into their fetters. Then begins an era of social revolution. The changes in the economic foundation lead sooner or later to the transformation of the whole immense superstructure. In studying such transformations it is always necessary to distinguish between the material transformation of the economic conditions of production, which can be determined with the precision of natural science, and the legal, political, religious, artistic or philosophic – in short, ideological forms in which men [*die Menschen*] become conscious of this conflict and fight it out. Just as one does not judge an individual by what he thinks about himself, so one cannot judge such a period of transformation by its consciousness, but, on the contrary, this consciousness must be explained from the contradictions of material life, from the conflict existing between the social forces of production and the relations of production.[158]

This suggests that agents' consciousness *cannot* be derived from their social existence "with the precision of natural science", that there is an element of open-endedness in agents' articulation of their experiences of and responses to their "lived" reality within the limits to the possible, with pressures and probabilities, set by the latter. Likewise, Engels wrote to Bloch that, "According to the materialist conception of history, the *ultimately* [*in letzter Instanz*] determining element in

---

[158] Marx, *A Contribution to the Critique of Political Economy*, p. 21 (*MEW*, 13, p. 9).

history is the production and reproduction of material life."[159]

If the determination of human agents' consciousness by their social existence is to be understood in a non-reductionist sense, as Marx' and Engels' words seem to indicate, and must in any case be assumed to be the case, then argument about the validity of opinions and theories is meaningful: agents may be persuaded by a better argument rather than their consciousness being the mere product of strict determination impervious to argument or logic.[160] And agents' articulation of their experiences of and responses to their "lived" reality cannot be *derived* from their social existence, which must be conceived as delimiting a field of the possible, with pressures and probabilities, in terms of this articulation.

The consequent distance between structural and historical analysis is reflected in the problem of class analysis, more precisely the problem of defining the capitalist working class and its boundaries. The capitalist relations of production, and hence the capitalist mechanism of appropriation of surplus value/labour, are fundamental in terms of grasping the nature of the capitalist type of society, capitalist class struggle, the developmental logic of the capitalist mode of production and type of society *and* the nature and fundamental class interest of the capitalist working class; and these are subjects of structural analysis. Whereas the capitalist working class as a *historical* phenomenon is one of historical analysis, in terms of

---

[159] Engels, "Engels an Joseph Bloch in Königsberg, 21./22. September 1890", p. 463.
[160] Cf. Favrholdt, p. 283. If the suggested interpretation of Marx' and Engels' words is correct, they contradict their expectations and predictions of the inevitable transition from capitalism to socialism and eventually classless communist society by the agency of the working class, thus demonstrating the tension in their historical materialism.

concrete actors (organisations, agents) articulating their experiences of and responses to their "lived" reality in all its concrete historical complexity, and as both an effect and a cause of its historical development.

Hence there can, again, be no *derivation* of these experiences and responses from the structural definition and analysis of the working class in terms of its position in the capitalist relations of production. However, if the boundaries of the class are drawn according to politico-ideological criteria, its structural basis in these relations of production is in effect overruled by those politico-ideological criteria. The definition as non-workers of groups of agents who, as non-owners of other means of production, have to offer their labour-power for sale because of their (prevalent) politico-ideological positions, although they share the fundamental working-class interest in a transition from capitalism to socialism and eventually classless communist society, is inconsistent.[161] And the more so as such politico-ideological positions develop over time: in the course of actual historical development, a process involving political and ideological struggles to influence agents' experiences and responses, whereas the fundamental positions in production defined by structural analysis remain the same. To expect agents' politico-ideological positions to be symmetrical with their positions in capitalist relations of production is thus simply unrealistic, implying as it does a straight determination of the former by the latter, neglecting or underrating the open-endedness and complexity of the process of actual historical development in the course of which agents' "lived" reality is formed and agents articulate their experiences of and responses to it.

---

[161] The cases of non-owners of means of production who are for various reasons enjoying such privileges that they do not, as individuals, have an objective (material) interest in a socialist transition are ignored here.

6. Discourse Analysis.

To avoid any misunderstanding to the effect that the emphasis on agency and agents' articulation of their experiences of and responses to their "lived" reality in any way amounts to a position cognate to discourse analysis or postmodernism, the following remarks seem appropriate before proceeding with the main subject.

The critique of Hindess & Hirst's *Pre-Capitalist Modes of Production* made by this writer in *A Critique of Mau:* Mute Compulsion *and Other Essays* should not require any further comments apart from a few on historical evidence, analysis and knowledge. Historical materialism obviously involves ideas about pre-capitalist history and transitions from one type of society to another in the past; Marx and Engels did indeed study, and write on, historical subjects; and historical writing and research involves the systematic testing of, and inferences from, historical evidence, including the *dialogue* between this evidence and theories and hypotheses,[162] and evaluations of the degree of certainty of its results. *Of course*, the study of history cannot be reduced to *either* the observation of the past as such, by means of some mysterious bypassing of the evidence, *or* the mere reading of a historiography which is "determined by the content of the various ideological forms which operate within the parameters of historical knowledge", so that, according to Hindess & Hirst,

> [.....]. History is a potentially infinite text, constantly doubling back on itself, constantly being re-written. Marxist history in no sense escapes from these limitations. It cannot transform the conditions of the historian's practice without ceasing to be history, and if it respects these conditions then it must be merely

---

[162] Cf. Thompson, *The Poverty of Theory and Other Essays*, p. 40.

another form of rationalising an object which it constitutes as the given. If Marxism gives us another history, if it recognises new representations as pertinent (the record of the class struggle, the aspirations of the masses, the evolution of material production, etc.), if it brings new ideological concerns to create, select and order the facts it will take as a given, then it merely gives us *another* history – a novel history, perhaps, but a history like all other histories.[163]

Against this, one may quote part of what was quoted from Hexter in *Experience and Historical Materialism*[164] as part of the argument against the relativism postulated by Keith Jenkins:

> [.....] there are no such things as radical or conservative questions about evidence and proof. Historical evidence is slight or abundant, dubious or trustworthy. Historical proof is difficult or easy, adequate or inadequate. Evidence and proof are never radical or conservative. Rather, they are part of the common language in which historians communicate with each other, the common ground on which they stand or fall. They are part of the discipline which, soon or late, the society of historians imposes on *all* its members.[165]

This does not mean that every controversy about history, whether turning on the nature of the process of historical development or the course of some specific chain of historical events and its causes and consequences, or whatever, is or can be solved by means of historical evidence and the facts inferable from it: the *interpretation* of historical evidence and facts, the actual developments and events insofar as they can

---

[163] Hindess & Hirst, p. 311.
[164] Gram-Jensen, *Experience and Historical Materialism*, p. 276-278.
[165] Hexter, p. 100.

be inferred from the evidence (*what* happened?) may also depend on the strength of various theories about the nature of society and historical development (*why* did it happen and with what consequences?). Such theories – for example Marx' and Engels' historical materialism or the revised version suggested here – are tested by the degree to which they serve, by means of the dialogue between theory and evidence, to make the best sense of developments in the past and present the records of which are in their turn found to be parts or examples of "the best and most likely account of the past that can be sustained by the relevant extrinsic evidence".[166] Or as Thompson wrote on historical evidence as a means of testing accounts of the past:

> [.....] Historical evidence has determinate properties. While any number of questions may be put to it, only certain questions will be appropriate. While any theory of historical process may be proposed, all theories are false which are not in conformity with the evidence's determinations. Herein lies the disciplinary court of appeal. In this sense it is true (we may agree here with Popper) that while historical knowledge must always fall short of positive proof (of the kinds appropriate to experimental science), false historical knowledge is generally subject to *dis*proof.[167]

The evidence may turn out to be too scanty, and/or the theories to be too inadequate for a definite settlement of the dispute to be arrived at, just as some parties may refuse to yield to the better argument; but the point is that rational argument about the relative merits of rival accounts of the past is *possible*: it is *not* a mere matter of choosing between rival ideologies, and history is *not* a potentially infinite text open to

---

166 Hexter, p. 55.
167 Thompson, *The Poverty of Theory and Other Essays*, p. 39-40.

arbitrary interpretation and re-writing as postulated by Hindess & Hirst.

Two points are worth making here. Firstly, the idea of *evidence* as the basis of, and control on, historical interpretation and theories is found in historians on both sides of the boundary of historical materialism.[168] Secondly, the meaning of any text – "text" in the sense of anything conveying some meaning – will be *more or less* fixed by its determinate properties. If this were not so, if *any* text or discourse could be interpreted in *any* way one chooses, the very idea of interpreting them would be meaningless: their determinate properties is what allows them to carry any meaning at all, precisely because these properties *set limits* to the range of interpretations which are not gainsaid by some property or properties of the text such as e. g. the presence of the word "not" at a specific point in a written text, or the specific arrangement and properties of images painted on a canvas.[169] Indeed, in one of their more sober moments, Laclau & Mouffe recognised this:

> [.....]. The impossibility of an ultimate fixity of meaning implies that there have to be partial fixations – otherwise, the very flow of differences would be impossible. Even in order to differ, to subvert meaning, there has to be *a* meaning. [.....] Any discourse is constituted as an attempt to dominate the field of discursivity, to

---

[168] Cf. Thompson, *The Poverty of Theory and Other Essays*, p. 40, note 37 referring to Hexter; and p. 41: "The appeal is not (or is rarely) to a choice of values, but to the logic of the discipline. And if we deny the determinate properties of the object, then no discipline remains."

[169] Cf. Evans, p. 120-121: "If a letter from an industrialist says he does not want any crystallization of the bourgeois right and the Nazis, then no amount of theorizing will alter that fact, and there is no way round it." Cf. Gram-Jensen, *Experience and Historical Materialism*, p. 62-64.

arrest the flow of differences, to construct a centre. We will call the privileged discursive points of this partial fixation, *nodal points*. [.....] – a discourse incapable of generating any fixity of meaning is the discourse of the psychotic.[170]

The degree of *precision* or *unambiguousness* of a text may thus be considered directly proportional to, and the effect of, the limitation its determinate properties impose on the reading of it. And at the other extreme from perfect precision or unambiguousness the absence of *any* such limitation will render a text *meaningless* (rather than possible ways of reading it being infinite) because *no* kind of definite meaning can be identified from its properties, thus excluding *any* way of interpreting it. The implication of this is, then, that if postmodernist claims that texts can be read in an infinite number of ways[171] were true, no communication would indeed be possible, as no text would convey *any* identifiable meaning.

The reasons for rejecting post-structuralism as represented by Laclau & Mouffe, Jenkins and others should be clear from the chapters dealing with it in *Experience and Historical Materialism* and *Structure, Agency and Theory*. Basically, they are, firstly, that post-structuralism implies a self-defeating relativism;

---

[170] Laclau & Mouffe, *Hegemony and Socialist Strategy*, p. 112. Their (later?) distinction between the *existence* of things, from which nothing follows, and the *being* of things (that is, what things are, and what they mean), which is discursively constructed (Laclau & Mouffe, "Post-Marxism without Apologies", p. 82-92) needs not be discussed here. It may, however, be mentioned that the successful predictions in various fields of science, and the fact that some technologies work and some do not, indicate the extradiscursive determinate properties of the natural world (Favrholdt, p. 148. McIntyre, p. 170).

[171] Jenkins, p. 11: "In that sense we read the world as a text, and, logically, such readings are infinite."

and, secondly, that it cannot explain actual discourses, and hence historical development, except by referring to other discourses in an endless regress; and, thirdly, that its rejection of historical materialism is not based on any cogent argument, let alone one demonstrating its own superiority. It should be superfluous to deal with it again at great length.

For one thing, its rejection of determination in the last instance does not demonstrate that no conception of such determination is tenable, while the following argument in Cutler et al. is unconvincing:

> If we reject economism and if we take that rejection seriously, then the question of representation cannot arise. Political and cultural practices, issues, and struggles do not represent interests determined elsewhere, at the level of the economy. It follows that specific political forces, issues and struggles can no longer be interpreted as essentially representing something else. [.....] Class 'interests' are not given to politics and ideology by the economy. They arise within political practice and they are determined as an effect of definite modes of political practice. Political practice does not recognize class interests and then represent them: it constitutes the interests which it represents[172]

The problem with this argument is that it renders the actual "political and cultural practices, issues and struggles" unaccountable for; why do discourses articulate any such practices, issues and struggles, and specific varieties of them, in the first place, if there is actually nothing – no interests, issues and conflicts – to represent in discourses?

---

[172] Cutler et al., I, p. 236-237. Cf. Laclau & Mouffe, "Post-Marxism without Apologies", p. 96-97.

Laclau & Mouffe's distinction between the *existence* of things, from which nothing follows,[173] on the one hand, and their discursively articulated *being*, which gives to things their identity, determining, for example, whether a stone is a projectile or an object of aesthetic contemplation (or something else)[174] is pivotal to their "discourse-analytical" approach, but untenable, as the very concept of the existence of some physical object "implies that it is *something* (some *thing*) rather than *nothing*, and that it is something (*some* thing) rather than any *other* thing.[175] A stone may be a projectile or an object of aesthetic contemplation, a mountain may be protection from enemy attack or the place for a touring trip or the source for the extraction of minerals etcetera because of their given physical properties (size, weight, solidity etcetera etcetera), and the idea that what they are depends entirely on discursive articulation leads to absurdities. In *Hegemony and Socialist Strategy*, Laclau & Mouffe asserted that,

> [.....]. An earthquake or the falling of a brick is an event that certainly exists, in the sense that it occurs here and now, independently of my will. But whether their specificity as objects is constructed in terms of 'natural phenomena" or 'expressions of the wrath of God', depends upon the structuring of a discursive field. What is denied is not that such objects exist externally to thought, but the rather different assertion that they could constitute themselves as objects outside any discursive conditions of emergence.[176]

---

[173] Laclau & Mouffe, "Post-Marxism without Apologies", p. 91.

[174] Laclau & Mouffe, "Post-Marxism without Apologies", p. 82; cf. p. 89: "Human beings socially construct their world, and it is through this construction – always precarious and incomplete – that they give to a thing its *being*."

[175] Gram-Jensen, *Experience and Historical Materialism*, p. 193.

[176] Laclau & Mouffe, *Hegemony and Socialist Strategy*, p. 108.

If the last period was only meant to point out that what we think of such events depends on "discursive conditions", e. g. whether we think of them and their causes in terms of magic, religion or natural science, Laclau & Mouffe would have a point, though not a very original one. But obviously their distinction between existence and being goes much further than that: according to Laclau & Mouffe, the existence of the fall of the brick and of the earthquake respectively are given, extra-discursive *data*, from which, however, nothing follows. *What* they are, natural phenomena or expressions of the wrath of God (or something else) depends on discourse, and thus on "discursive conditions of emergence". Whether they are natural phenomena or expressions of the wrath of God (or something else) must, in its turn, imply that they have different causes, depending on the way human beings – we – socially construct their – our – world. As Laclau & Mouffe argued in their reply to Geras' critique of *Hegemony and Socialist Strategy*,

> [.....]. It would be absurd, of course, to ask oneself today if 'being a projectile' is part of the true being of the stone (although the question would have some legitimacy within Platonic metaphysics); the answer, obviously, would be: it depends on the way we use stones. For the same reason it would be absurd to ask oneself if, outside all scientific theory, atomic structure is the 'true being' of matter – the answer will be that atomic theory is a way we have of classifying certain objects, but that these are open to different forms of conceptualization that may emerge in the future. In other words, the 'truth', factual or otherwise, about the being of objects is constituted within a theoretical and discursive context, and the idea of a truth outside all context is simply nonsensical.[177]

---

[177] Laclau & Mouffe, "Post-Marxism without Apologies", p. 85-86.

Putting 'truth' in inverted commas in this passage is logical, as the obvious implication of Laclau & Mouffe's argument is that no way of classifying objects is more or less true than any other, "truth", whether taken in a literal or non-literal sense, being dependent on the discursive context. In other words, that the fall of a brick or an earthquake is a natural phenomenon or an expression of the wrath of God, and matter has or does not have an atomic structure according to whether they are conceptualised in one or the other way; which raises the question whether they are materially changed from one thing to another if (re-)conceptualised in a different way, and whether they can be both things at the same time, if conceptualised in different ways at the same time.

It should be obvious that this demonstrates that Laclau & Mouffe's discourse-analytical approach is a dead end: existence is in effect evacuated of any reality, having no consequences in terms of what things are and how they can be handled and related to, allowing the discursive articulation of the being of objects to be completely arbitrary, thus leaving the 'truth' about that being completely dependent on this arbitrary construction, that is, dissolving the very idea of any objective truth about the world.[178] In addition, this rejection of the idea of a truth outside all context as simply nonsensical logically implies that "the 'truth', factual or otherwise" of Laclau & Mouffe's own argument is just as dependent on its theoretical and discursive context, and is thus no more factual than any other, if their argument is accepted – that is, they are caught up in the self-refuting nature of relativism.[179]

---

[178] Cf. Geras, "Post-Marxism?", p. 67.
[179] As pointed out by Paul Boghossian, quoted in Evans, p. 220-221. Cf. Gram-Jensen, *Experience and Historical Materialism*, p. 283. Geras, "Ex-Marxism Without Substance", p. 59-60.

Taking a closer look at the statement on the falling of a brick and an earthquake, how can they be events occurring independently of human will, if nothing follows from existence, and they are nothing distinct from other kinds of events before being discursively articulated? Do they not occur from *causes*, which must be independent of the subsequent discursive articulation of them as either natural phenomena or expressions of the wrath of God or whatever else? What makes us classify them in one or the other way, if nothing in their existence separates them from everything else? Is human beings' discursive articulation of the being of things arbitrary? Or is it e. g. related to the effects of various different events, or the different materials, like blocks, pillars, slabs and beams or other things used, for example, to build a house?[180] Moreover, how can we say that "such objects exist externally to thought", or that, "If there were no human beings on earth, those objects that we call stones would be there nonetheless"[181] if nothing follows from their mere existence, and "it would be absurd to ask oneself if, outside all scientific theory, atomic theory is the 'true being' of matter – the answer will be that atomic theory is a way we have of classifying certain objects, but that these are open to different forms of conceptualization that may emerge in the future"?[182]

If objects of various kinds – such as stones distinguished from e. g. water or light – exist even in the absence of human agents to articulate their being discursively, then how can we

---

[180] Laclau & Mouffe argue that, "It is evident that the very material properties of objects are part of what Wittgenstein calls language game, which is an example of what we have called discourse." (*Hegemony and Socialist Strategy*, p. 108). And if nothing follows from the mere (pre- or extradiscursive) existence of things, these "material properties of objects" must be assumed to be given to them by discursive articulation – cf. "Post-Marxism without Apologies", p. 89.
[181] Laclau & Mouffe, "Post-Marxism without Apologies", p. 84.
[182] Laclau & Mouffe, "Post-Marxism without Apologies", p. 85-86.

indeed say that nothing follows from their mere existence, e. g. *how* they can or cannot be used in *material* practice by human beings which themselves have definite physical and mental properties? In other words, how can we deny that irreducible material properties of objects (and events) setting limits to the ways in which we can relate to them exist independently of discourse?[183] And that physical and psychological needs of human beings – and hence also human *interests* – may therefore be irreducible to mere articulation?[184]

In other words, the interaction between social circumstances and agency is irreducible to discursive articulation – although there is a discursive aspect to social practice inasmuch as we act on what we *think about* the world and our possibilities rather than on the objective facts about them – but may also be forced to revise what we think about them precisely because what we think about them on the one hand and the objective facts about them on the other may differ – with the objective facts rendering our attempts to handle our "lived" reality according to our wishes ineffective.

And the dead end of the discourse-analytical approach is not made any less obvious by Laclau & Mouffe's statement that, "Whenever we use the category of 'subject' in this text, we will do so in the sense of 'subject positions' within a discursive structure. Subjects cannot, therefore, be the origin of social relations – not even in the limited sense of being endowed with powers that render an experience possible – as all 'experience' depends on precise discursive conditions of

---

[183] Cf. the joke about building skyscrapers from the top down cited in Gram-Jensen, *Structure, Agency and Theory*, p. 235.
[184] Human beings may, for example, die if certain biologically given needs are not fulfilled, and no kind of discursive articulation has hitherto been demonstrated to make them stay alive without food and drink.

possibility."[185] Which implies the absolute primacy of discourse, that discourses construct agents as 'subject positions' in specific discourses, thus giving "agents" their being, rather than agents articulating discourses. Which, in its turn, is confirmed by Laclau & Mouffe's inability to explain the emergence of new discourses – more precisely discourses articulating resistance to women's subordination – in terms of social conditions, which reduces them to referring to the – in its turn unaccounted-for – emergence of "democratic discourse" as "the new matrix of the social imaginary".[186]

This reduction of historical development to a process of unaccountably emerging self-articulating discourses substituting themselves for others may, finally, be considered the logical terminal point of the "retreat from class", as Meiksins Wood has aptly termed it,[187] a movement away from accounting for historical development in terms of the interaction between social circumstances and agency towards the primacy and autonomy of discourse the direction of which is discernible form the following words of Paul Hirst:

> It follows that the notion of *relative* autonomy is untenable. Once any degree of autonomous action is accorded to political forces as means of representation *vis-à-vis* classes of economic agents, then there is no necessary correspondence between the forces that appear in the political (and what they 'represent') and economic classes. It is not simply a question of discrepancy (the political means 'represent' the class more or less accurately) but of necessary non-correspondence. One cannot, despite Lenin, 'read back' – measuring the political forces against what they are

---

[185] Laclau & Mouffe, *Hegemony and Socialist Strategy*, p. 115.
[186] Laclau & Mouffe, *Hegemony and Socialist Strategy*, p. 154-155.
[187] Meiksins Wood, *The Retreat from Class*.

supposed to represent. That is to conceive the represented as external to, as the autonomously existent measure of, its means of representation. Classes do not have given 'interests', apparent independently of definite parties, ideologies, etc., and against which these parties, ideologies, etc. can be measured. What the means of representation 'represent' does not exist outside the process of representation. The 'represented' carries no sign, no means of recognition, other than that constituted by its means of representation. The issues, the ideologies the classes specified within the political arena are constituted there – one cannot read back beyond it to some essential arena of class struggle beyond politics. That is what is meant by non-correspondence.[188]

As pointed out by Meiksins Wood, this critique of "representation" is "not supported by empirical investigation or historical evidence."[189] Apart from the historical connection between the growth and development of the capitalist working class on the one hand and that of political struggles and organisations and ideologies on the other, the conflict of interests between capitalists and workers can, as noted above, be derived from the analysis of capital(ism) on trivial assumptions about human beings' physical and psychological needs.[190] And there is no reason why we should have to accept the premise that, "Once any degree of autonomous action is accorded to political forces as means of representation *vis-à-vis* classes of economic agents, then there is no necessary correspondence between the forces that appear in the

[188] Paul Hirst, p. 130-131. Cf. Cutler et al., p. 384-387 (quoted in Gram-Jensen, *Experience and Historical Materialism*, p. 198-199) and Laclau & Mouffe, *Hegemony and Socialist Strategy*, p. 83-84, p. 120; "Post-Marxism without Apologies", p. 96-97.
[189] Meiksins Wood, *The Retreat from Class*, p. 79-80.
[190] Cf. Wright, *Classes*, p. 28, p. 36.

political (and what they 'represent') and economic classes." The connection, or (more or less accurate) correspondence or representation may perfectly well be conceived of as one of structural determination or determination "in the last instance",[191] that is, as one of the class structure "setting the limits of possible variation of class formation, class consciousness and class struggle."[192] These limits may well turn out to be wider than often assumed, depending on the precise historical conditions and the ways agents handle their "lived" reality and wage ideological and political struggles over the articulation of their experiences of and responses to it, but the assertion that we have to choose between either total determination or total autonomy has not been made good by either Hirst, Cutler et al. or Laclau or Mouffe or, for that matter, Jenkins. As pointed out before, the ultimate consequence of their rejection of determination is exemplified in Jenkins' "postmodern" reply to Perez Zagorin:

> [.....] it is this point – that we are all antifoundationalists now – that Zagorin just cannot get. This is illustrated when he plays what I have already referred to as an apparent trump card: that the "skepticism" and relativism postmodernists champion undercuts – if only they knew it – their own positions. But of course they do know it. And they don't care. Because it doesn't matter. For what worries Zagorin – that without foundations you are too weak to rebuff or refute foundational opponents – misses the point that there aren't any credible foundational opponents around any more. Postmodernists are not weak because they have no foundations because nobody has foundations; we are all relativists now, all postmodernists now.

---

[191] Engels, "Engels an Joseph Bloch in Königsberg, 21./22. September 1890", p. 463.
[192] Wright, *Classes*, p. 28.

Accordingly, it is at this point that we arguably reach not only the end of history but the end of ethics too (in the sense that philosophy could ostensibly ground *the* ethical code) and emerge foundationally naked into the world of the politics of hegemony. Ernesto Laclau has seen this more clearly than most:

> The metaphysical [logocentric] discourse of the West is coming to an end, and philosophy in its twilight has performed a last service for us in the deconstruction of its own terrain. Let us think, for instance, of Derrida's undecidables. Once undecidability has reached the ground itself – once the organisation of a certain camp is governed by a hegemonic decision – hegemonic because it is not objectively determined, because different decisions were also possible – the realm of philosophy comes to an end and the realm of politics begins. This realm will be inhabited by a different type of discourse ... which ... constructs the world on the "grounds" of a radical undecidability.[193]

Ultimately, the logical implication of the assumptions or postulates on which the case for the discourse-analytical approach is based is that we cannot say anything the validity or invalidity of which can be demonstrated about extra-discursive reality, as "the 'truth', factual or otherwise, about the being of objects is constituted within a theoretical and discursive context, and the idea of a truth outside all context is

---

[193] Jenkins, *At the Limits of History*, p. 103 (quoting from Laclau, *Emancipations* (London, Verso, 1996), p. 123). Cf. Gram-Jensen, *A Critique of Mau: Mute Compulsion and Other Essays*, p.180-183. Cf. Geras, "Post-Marxism?" p. 75-78.

simply nonsensical."[194] On that assumption all we can do is to make arbitrary choices between different (thus, in terms of validation/truth, circular) discourses – that is, if we can indeed do that much, considering Laclau & Mouffe's assertion that, "Subjects cannot, therefore, be the origin of social relations – not even in the limited sense of being endowed with powers that render an experience possible – as all 'experience' depends on precise discursive conditions of possibility."[195] According to this, everything is discourse, and discourse is everything.

As far as the conception of the interaction between social circumstances and agency as the motive power of historical development and transformations is concerned, and the crucial role which agents' articulation of their experiences of and responses to their "lived" reality is assumed to play in that development, it is essential to emphasise that this has *nothing* whatsoever to do with any discourse-theoretical ideas to the effect that, "the 'truth', factual or otherwise, about the being of objects is constituted within a theoretical and discursive context, and the idea of any truth outside all context is simply nonsensical",[196] or that, "Human beings socially construct their world, and it is through this construction – always precarious and incomplete – that they give to a thing its being",[197] let alone that, "Whenever we use the category of 'subject' [.....], we will do so in the sense of 'subject positions'

---

[194] Laclau & Mouffe, "Post-Marxism without Apologies", p. 86. It is strange that Laclau & Mouffe, who affirmed "the *material* character of every discursive structure" in *Hegemony and Socialist Strategy* (p. 108), fail to realise that some "theoretical and discursive contexts", including theories about the being of things, can be validated *materially*, either by experiment or by the fact that technology based on them *works* (cf. Favrholdt, p. 148).

[195] Laclau & Mouffe, *Hegemony and Socialist Strategy*, p. 115.

[196] Laclau & Mouffe, "Post-Marxism without Apologies", p. 86.

[197] Laclau & Mouffe, "Post-Marxism without Apologies", p. 89.

within a discursive structure. Subjects cannot, therefore, be the origin of social relations – not even in the limited sense of being endowed with powers that render an experience possible – as all 'experience' depends on precise discursive conditions of possibility."[198] Apart from the first quoted passage being self-refuting, the second and the third ones being somewhat contradictory insofar as human beings are in effect reduced to "subject positions" within discursive structures, while the implication of the third one is that changes in discursive positions of possibility and hence of "subject positions" and "experiences" are unaccountable for, because changes in discourses can only be "explained" by reference to other discourses,[199] nobody who has bothered to read the arguments on the discourse-analytical approach of Laclau & Mouffe and Keith Jenkins in the books by this writer[200] should be able to overlook the distance between that approach and the historical-materialist position of the latter.

This does *not* mean that this writer supports any idea that agents' social circumstances determine agent's articulation of their experiences and responses in more than a general sense, reducing the field of the possible to only *one* potential outcome. Marx' dictum that, "It is not the consciousness of men that determines their existence, but their social existence that determines their consciousness"[201] is unobjectionable as long as it is understood in a non-reductionist sense: agents' social existence is *what is there* for agents to experience and respond to, including the specific *conditions* for their articulation of

---

[198] Laclau & Mouffe, *Hegemony and Socialist Strategy*, p. 115.

[199] Cf. Laclau & Mouffe on "The Democratic Revolution", *Hegemony and Socialist Strategy*, p.152 ff.

[200] Gram-Jensen, *Experience and Historical Materialism*, fourth and fifth essays; *Structure, Agency and Theory*, Part Two, ch. 4; *A Critique of Mau: Mute Compulsion and Other Essays*, sixth essay.

[201] Marx, *A Contribution to the Critique of Political Economy*, p. 21 (*MEW*, 13, p. 9).

their experiences and responses, conditions obviously *also*, and importantly, determined by their given positions in the relations of production. But the individual lives and social circumstances of all kinds of agents will tend to make their precise conditions for articulating them more or less different, and even disregarding this it cannot be taken for granted that similar circumstances will inevitably produce similar experiences and responses. The position adopted here rests on the assumption – which everyday as well as historical experience certainly seems to confirm – that agents' articulation of their experiences of and responses to their "lived" reality is a matter of structural determination in Wright's sense,[202] implying the open-ended nature of the process of agents' articulation of their experiences of and responses to their "lived" reality (open-ended, that is, within limits set by the social structure and the actual outcomes of historical development, the delimitation of a field of the possible with pressures and probabilities), and hence of the process of historical development itself. As it has been put, "determination works as the setting of limits, a 'repertoire' of possible outcomes to any situation."[203] It only remains to be emphasised that *all* the factors which are parts of the reality of the situation in question contribute to the limitation, the exertion of pressures and thus the relative probability of the possible outcomes.[204] The past determines the present, and the present determines the future in this Wrightean sense. A position one implication of which is, again, that we should *neither* assume that anything goes, *nor* that what we think and do makes no real difference.

---

[202] Wright, *Class, Crisis and the State*, p. 15-17. Cf. Gram-Jensen, *Structure, Agency and Theory*, Part Two, ch. 1, and p. 1328 (Determination in the last instance); *Experience and Historical Materialism*, third essay, sections b and d, especially p. 177-178; *A Revised Historical Materialism*, first essay, section c.

[203] Gray, p. 173.

[204] Cf. Gray, ibid.

One reason why anything does not go, why the process of agents' – our – articulation of experiences and responses cannot be considered arbitrary is simply that it is part of, and conditioned by, our practical and material handling of, and relationship with, social reality, which includes material reality. Thus, there are biological needs and conditions which we cannot escape, and material conditions for and consequences of human practice. As only too obviously demonstrated by, for example, climate change. For this reason, Thompson's warning not to overlook "the *dialogue* between social being and social consciousness"[205] should be taken heed of: the articulation of social consciousness is irreducible to a mere reflection of social being, but it does not take place in isolation from it: it is interacting with it, indeed part of it, an aspect of our *handling* of our social being. And for this reason, and being irreducible to a mere reflection of social being, ideological struggles may make a difference, but cannot, at the same time, be assumed to do so arbitrarily: it seems a reasonable assumption that ideology, in the sense of a more or less coherent system of ideas and notions, has to seem to *make sense* of agents' given "lived" reality in order to persuade them.

Agents' articulation of experiences and responses is part of, and reflecting, the *concrete* process of historical development, and both one of the causes (or co-determinants) of this development and an effect of it. It cannot be taken for granted that class relations or structural developments are inevitably uppermost in the minds of agents and thus primary conditions of, and reflected in, their experiences and responses at any given moment. While these relations and developments are important conditions of agents' "lived" reality, they are not necessarily *experienced*, let alone *responded to*, as such. Other factors, such as e. g. (the effects of) economic conjunctures or war or peace may be experienced as important in their own

---

[205] Thompson, *The Poverty of Theory and Other Essays*, p. 9.

right, isolated from their structural context, and, again, ideological and political struggles must be taken into account.

Rather than positing that laws of historical development comparable to those of natural developments determine the will, consciousness and intentions of agents,[206] we should think of the process of agents' articulation of their experiences of and responses to their "lived" reality as one in which they – we – have to *find out* who they – we – are, what their – our – situation is, and what can and should be done about it. That is, if we are serious about rejecting the idea of agents' – our – consciousness as a reflection of reality, we have to realise that our articulation of our experiences of and responses to our "lived" reality is nothing but our *more or less* systematic endeavour to make sense of this reality and find out what to think and do about it. And the only ideational tools and knowledge available to us apart from those won in the course of this endeavour itself are those inherited from the past, which we have to test and improve as part of the endeavour. We do not passively receive our experiences and responses, our consciousness, from our "lived" reality – we articulate our experiences of and responses to that reality within the limits imposed by its objective nature which sets the conditions for making sense of it and handling it. Thus, the process is a mental *and* practical one of trial and error throughout our lifetimes, and continuing from generation to generation.[207]

Agents' articulation of their experiences of and responses to their "lived" reality must be considered an integral part of their very social existence, an ongoing process which is partly

[206] Marx, *Das Kapital*, 1, p. 26.

[207] We are of course subjected to processes of socialization from our birth and throughout life, but whatever conceptions and ideas we acquire through these processes they will still be tested against our "lived" reality, in terms of whether or not they can help us make (what seems to be) sense of this reality.

unconscious, conditioned by their social positions as well as their upbringing and education and the totality of their human relations and connections as well as their individual courses of life, which are bound up with the contemporary historical development, and of course traditions and norms, inherited and developing, and the experiences and responses of the preceding generations. A process including their development of (both explicit and implicit) value systems, tastes, preferences, antipathies, self-evaluation, patterns of behaviour in different situations and towards different people.[208]

What the process is *not* is the simple, automatic *reflection* of social reality in agents' brains, or the automatic imposition of specific individualities on them by the social structure according to its needs. Again, agents – *we* – have to find out, they – we – *respond to* their – our – "lived" reality, in a constant process the further development of which will be structurally determined by its past stages. Responses may not be *totally* conscious, but they will nevertheless shape agents as individuals, and hence their further articulation of their experiences of and responses to their "lived" reality. We cannot take it for granted that we are fully aware of our own individualities or patterns of responding, or fully understand them. The effects of our "lived" reality are hardly fully known by ourselves, but they must nevertheless be considered real, and reflected by our practical and emotional reactions.

If it is true that we act on what we *think about* the world and our possibilities rather than on the objective facts about them,[209] then the importance of our articulation of our experiences of and responses to our "lived" reality, and of articulating them in as close an approximation as possible to the objective facts about our world and our possibilities is

---

[208] Cf. Bourdieu.
[209] Gram-Jensen, *Structure, Agency and Theory*, p. 15.

obvious. In sharp contradistinction from Engels' notion of agents' wills cancelling out and thus allowing the course of history to unfold according to laws comparable to those ruling natural processes, as well as from Marx' similar (though still different) notion of history being ruled by laws of development of the same quasi-natural kind determining agents' will, consciousness and intentions.

So, to conclude on this and avoid a possible misunderstanding: we do indeed act on what we *think about* the world and our possibilities rather than on the objective facts about them, but this has to be understood in the right way: what we think about the world and our possibilities has to be to some extent *correct* if we are to survive in the world with our given possibilities. Fulfilling our physical and psychological needs, and thus securing our survival, requires a minimum of know-how; we are ourselves *part of*, and *depend on*, the world in its physical reality and have to adapt to, and *handle*, that physical reality. This also requires that we are able to think and *communicate* about it – which exerts a pressure on the way in which we develop our language and think and speak/communicate about the world, and requires that we revise what we think about the world and our possibilities if what we think about them turns out, in practice, to be wrong.[210]

It should be superfluous to argue at any great length that this is a condition for our more or less effective handling of our natural and social reality, and for technological development, and thus limits *arbitrariness* of language and consciousness. And contradicts the idea of distinguishing between the *existence* of things, from which nothing follows, on the one hand and the *being* of things, which is (precariously) discursively

---

[210] Cf. Favrholdt, p. 349, p. 351, p. 357-358, p. 366-367 and ch. XIII, passim.

constructed, on the other, the 'truth', factual or not, thus being dependent on discursive articulation.

Thus, the suggested revised historical materialism (a suggestion leaving wide scope for different ideas about what it should amount to) still is, and must be, a *materialism*: it confirms the irreducibility of reality to discursive articulation or consciousness. The world has a material, physical existence/reality which is prior to and independent of what we think about it, and can never, however we think about it and *handle* it, be reduced to discursive articulation or human consciousness.

7. Laws Of Historical Development?

As one of the elements of what he considered "vulgar Marxism", Hobsbawm mentioned, in a text written for a symposium held in May 1968,[211]

> 'Historical laws and historical inevitability'. It was believed, correctly, that Marx insisted on a systematic and necessary development of human society in history, from which the contingent was largely excluded, at all events at the level of generalization about long-term movements. Hence the constant preoccupation of early Marxist writers on history with such problems as the role of the individual or of accident in history. On the other hand this could be, and largely was, interpreted as a rigid and imposed regularity, for example in the succession of socio-economic formations, or even a mechanical determinism which sometimes came close to suggesting that there was no alternatives in history.[212]

The question whether there is a tension, or contradiction, between Engels' notion of agents' wills cancelling out – or the idea of historical development ruled by laws determining the will, consciousness and intentions of agents – on the one hand and his vision of the realm of freedom[213] on the other may be left aside here. What is certain is the tension between the former and the emphasis on human beings' conscious relation to their own life which distinguishes them from (other) animals.[214] Or, expressed somewhat differently, but essentially concerning the same issue, the tension between the

---

[211] Hobsbawm, *On History*, p. 186.
[212] Hobsbawm, *On History*, p. 192-193.
[213] Engels, *Anti-Dühring*, p. 335-336 (*MEW*, 20, p. 264).
[214] Marx, *Early Writings*, p. 328-329 (*MEW*, Ergänzungsband, erster Teil, p. 516-517).

conception of historical development as a quasi-natural process ruled by laws independent of the will, consciousness and intentions of human beings (which are, on the contrary, according to the Russian reviewer whose words Marx endorsed as an accurate depiction of his, Marx', "real method", "the dialectical method",[215] determined by these laws) on the one hand and that of human beings as the makers of their own history under given and inherited circumstances, history as nothing but human beings pursuing their own ends under these circumstances, on the other.

A central element in the suggested revision of historical materialism is, of course, precisely the elimination of this tension by means of the rejection of the determinist tendency in Marx and Engels in its various shapes: that is, the rejection of the conception of the dialectic of forces and relations of production as the motive power of historical development and transformations, of the notion of agents' wills cancelling out or being determined by quasi-natural laws and of the very tendency to think of historical development as a lawed process comparable to those of natural development generally.

If this tendency is rejected, the will, consciousness and intentions of human agents must be considered a crucial determinant of the process of historical development in which it interacts with social circumstances – in accordance with that other tendency in Marx' and Engels' historical materialism, the emphasis on human beings' conscious relation to their own life, and on these same human beings as the makers of their own history under the given and inherited circumstances, including that tradition of the dead generations which weighs like a nightmare on the minds of the living. The wills, the different forms of consciousness and the intentions of human agents do not cancel out, they compete

---

[215] Marx, *Das Kapital*, 1, p. 27.

with each other for influence on the articulation of experiences of and responses to agents' "lived" reality, and thus on agents' *handling* of that reality. The ensuing interaction between agency and social circumstances is the motive power of historical development, including historical transformations.

Above, Marx' and Engels' ideas about certain laws of historical development and transformations were discussed and rejected. Marx did, as we have seen, make the reservation that all laws are modified in their eventuation "by manifold circumstances",[216] but as the textual evidence makes abundantly clear, he and Engels made no such reservation in the case of their expectations and predictions about the inevitability of the transition from capitalism to socialism and eventually classless communist society based on their conception of the dialectic of forces and relations of production as the motive power of historical development and transformations, nor did the reservation stop them from positing quasi-natural laws determining the will, consciousness and intentions of agents, or more generally ruling historical development as a (quasi-)natural process.

What remains to be considered before turning to the implications of the rejection of the idea of the inevitability of this transition, and that of such quasi-natural laws of development, is the question whether the *general* idea of laws of historical development is tenable.

In a lecture entitled "Has History Made Progress?" given in 1979,[217] Hobsbawm has observed that, "history has moved away from description and narrative to analysis and explanation; from concentrating on the unique and individual to

---

[216] Marx, *Das Kapital*, 1, p. 674; cf. 3, p. 799-800, p. 839.
[217] Hobsbawm, *On History*, p. 74.

establishing regularities and to generalization." This, he declared, constitutes progress,[218] but he also made the reservation that human beings "are different as well as similar to animals" because,

> They make their own world and their own history. This evidently does not mean that they are free to do so as they consciously choose (whatever 'conscious choice' means), or that history can be understood by investigating men's intentions. It clearly can't. But it does mean that the transformations of human society are mediated by a number of phenomena which are specifically human (let's call them 'culture' in the widest sense of the word) and they operate through a number of institutions and practices which are at least in part conscious constructs – for instance, governments and policies. We can both construct and move about this furniture of human life among which we live – to what extent is one of the bigger historical questions – and, since we have language, we always have and express ideas about ourselves and our activities.
>
> [.....]. What I am saying is that history can't leave out consciousness, culture and purposive action within man-made institutions.[219]

In a similar vein, Evans has argued that,

> [.....]. Yet history clearly includes the study of individual people, events and structures as well as groups and collectivities. The differences that exist between two human beings, even when they live in the same time and place, are vastly more complex than the

---

[218] Hobsbawm, *On History*, p. 84.
[219] Hobsbawm, *On History*, p. 86.

differences between two atoms or two molecules. Human individuality is far greater than microbial individuality. This makes the framing of general laws to cover it correspondingly far more difficult.[220]

Evans has argued that historians should try to make generalisations rather than propounding laws of history, the difference between generalisations and laws being that laws do not permit exceptions, whereas generalisations do.[221]

> History, then, can produce generalizations, though the broader they are, the more exceptions there are likely to be and the further removed they will become from hard evidence which can be cited in their support. Its objects of study are in no sense confined to discrete individuals or events. It can identify, or posit with a high degree of plausibility, trends and structures in the human past. In these respects it can legitimately be regarded as scientific. But history cannot create laws with predictive power. An understanding of the past might help in the present insofar as it broadens our knowledge of human nature, provides us with an inspiration – or a warning – or suggests plausible, though always fallible arguments about the likely possibilities of certain things happening under certain conditions. None of this, however, comes anywhere near the immutable predictive certainty of a scientific law. All those who thought, or claimed, that they had discovered laws in history, from Marx and Engels to Toynbee and Buckle, were wrong; indeed, as we have seen, as soon as Marxists in Russia thought they recognized

---

[220] Evans, p. 57-58.
[221] Evans, p. 58-59.

a historical law, they proceeded to do their level best to break it.[222]

At the bottom of this is the fact that the same human agency which is the necessary condition for the existence of historical development of human society, the motive power of which is the interaction between social circumstances and agency, renders the establishment of laws of historical development comparable to those ruling natural processes (such as those of classical physics) impossible.

We may of course learn various – and sometimes important – lessons about historical development, modes of production, mechanisms of exploitation, social conflicts and struggles, transformations, failed or successful strategies, etcetera from the historical record. The study of history is not, *pace* Hindess & Hirst,[223] valueless for theoretical development or practice in the current situation. This is indeed part of the stuff of the present text too. But such experience is not the same as the establishment of laws of historical development, or the demonstration of laws comparable to those of natural development.

Although the current situation (conjuncture), itself brought about by the interaction between social circumstances and agency, will inevitably delimit a field of the possible with pressures and probabilities in terms of agents' articulation of their experiences of and responses to their "lived" reality, and hence the ensuing historical development, a "lawed" process of historical development would require that agents' will, consciousness and intentions are either determined by quasi-natural laws of historical development *or* cancel out, so that

---

[222] Evans, p. 60-61.
[223] "The study of history is not only scientifically but also politically valueless." Hindess & Hirst, p. 312.

historical development is in effect a process independent of human agency, as human agents are its mere bearers or supports. As this is unrealistic, leaving the very fact of historical development unaccounted for, the notion of it as a process ruled by (quasi-natural) laws must be rejected as untenable. And hence Popper's argument against the predictability of historical development: that, *"we cannot anticipate today what we shall know only tomorrow"*[224] may be supplemented with the similar one that we cannot anticipate future articulations of experiences and responses.

It may be added that if human actors are able to relate to and handle their "lived" reality, that is, articulating their experiences of and responses to it, among other things handling it by means of technological development, there is no need to assume either laws of historical development or some (divine?) *telos* of historical development and transformations ruling the process with human agents as mere bearers or supports. Such ideas must be considered quasi-religious speculations. If Marx had stuck consistently to his understanding of historical development as the interaction between social circumstances and agency, agents' *handling* of their "lived" reality, that is, all naturally and socially given circumstances affecting them, his and Engels' conceptions of history as a quasi-natural process ruled by quasi-natural laws of development would have been superfluous; just as their conception of the dialectic of forces and relations of production as the motive power of historical development and transformations guaranteeing the transition from capitalism to socialism and eventually classless communist society would have been both superfluous and devoid of any foundation.

Where is that understanding of Marx' stated? In his *Economic and Philosophical Manuscripts* written 1844, where, making the

---

[224] Popper, *The Poverty of Historicism*, p. vii.

same distinction between human beings on the one hand and animals on the other as Hobsbawm, he wrote that,

> The animal is immediately one with its life activity. It is not distinct from that activity; it *is* that activity. Man [*der Mensch*] makes his life activity itself an object of his will and consciousness. He has conscious life activity. It is not a determination with which he directly merges. Conscious life activity directly distinguishes man from animal life activity. Only because of that is he a species-being. Or rather, he is a conscious being, i.e. his own life is an object for him, only because he is a species-being. Only because of that is his activity free activity.[225]

And that,

> It is therefore in his fashioning of the objective world that man really proves himself to be a *species-being*. Such production is his active species-life. Through it nature appears as *his* work and his reality. The object of labour is therefore the *objectification of the species-life of man*: for man reproduces himself not only intellectually, in his consciousness, but actively and actually, and he can therefore contemplate himself in a world he himself has created. In tearing away the object of his production from man, estranged labour therefore tears away from him his *species-life*, his true species-objectivity, and transforms his advantage over animals into the disadvantage that his inorganic body, nature, is taken away from him.[226]

---

[225] Marx, *Early Writings*, p. 328 (*MEW*, Ergänzungsband, erster Teil, p. 516).
[226] Marx, *Early Writings*, p. 329 (*MEW*, Ergänzungsband, erster Teil, p. 517 (the word "world" after "objective" is missing in the former).

The notion of human agents' specifically *conscious* handling of their "lived" reality, their interaction with their given natural and social circumstances, is also found in *Capital*:

> Labour is, in the first place, a process between man and nature, a process in which man effects, regulates and controls his metabolism with nature through his own activity. [.....] Acting on external nature and changing it through this movement, he simultaneously changes his own nature. He develops the potentialities dormant in him and subjects the play of their powers to his own control. We are not dealing with the first animal-like instinctive forms of labour here. [.....] We presuppose labour in a form in which it belongs exclusively to man. A spider carries out operations resembling those of a weaver, and a bee puts many a human builder to shame in the construction of her wax cells. But what from the outset distinguishes the poorest builder from the best bee is that he has constructed the cell in his mind before he constructs it in wax. At the end of the labour-process a result appears which even at its beginning was present in the worker's imagination, i.e., already ideally. [227]

In addition to this, Marx and Engels rejected teleological-functionalist conceptions of history and the reduction of human agents to the mere bearers or supports of its development towards its *telos*:

> [.....]. *History* does *nothing*, it "owns *no* immense riches", it "fights *no* battles"! On the contrary it is *man* [*der Mensch*], real, living man, who does, owns and fights all of it; it is hardly "history" that uses man as a means of

---

[227] Marx, *Das Kapital*, 1, p. 192-193.

going through with *its* ends – as if it were a person apart – rather it is *nothing* but the activity of man pursuing his own ends.[228]

History is nothing but the succession of the separate generations, each of which exploits the materials, the capital funds, the productive forces handed down to it by all preceding generations, and thus, on the one hand, continues the traditional activity in completely changed circumstances and, on the other, modifies the old circumstances with a completely changed activity. This can be speculatively distorted so that later history is made the goal of earlier history, e.g., the goal ascribed to the discovery of America is to further the eruption of the French Revolution. Thereby history receives its own special aims and becomes "a person ranking with other persons" [.....], while what is designated with the words "destiny", "goal", "germ", or "idea" of earlier history is nothing more than an abstraction formed from later history, from the active influence which earlier history exercises on later history.[229]

The tension in their historical materialism is unmistakable when considering the distance between these passages on the one hand and e. g. the "15 sentences" in Marx' 1859 Preface to *A Contribution to the Critique of Political Economy*, his quotation from the Russian reviewer in his 1873 Afterword to the 2nd edition of *Capital*, or Engels' words about human wills cancelling out in his 1890 letter to Bloch, especially when one considers that the conception of the dialectic of forces and relations of production as the motive power of historical

---

[228] Marx & Engels, *Die heilige Familie*, p. 98.
[229] Marx & Engels, *Die deutsche Ideologie*, p. 45. Cf. Engels, *Anti-Dühring*, Part I, ch. VII.

development and transformations is already found in *Die deutsche Ideologie* written 1845-46. But the main point here is that if the (non-teleological) process of historical development is *nothing* but the activity of human agents pursuing their own ends, there are no laws ruling this process of historical development guaranteeing that it will proceed according to the assumed dialectic of forces and relations of production, or towards a predictable outcome, although the ends and activities of human agents will always be conditioned by the given circumstances of the conjuncture or current situation.

8. Laws of History in Marx and Engels.

It is hardly possible to draw up a logically consistent formula expressing Marx' and Engels' conception of the relationship between laws of historical development and agency, simply because they never arrived at any logically consistent conception; which must, in its turn, in the final analysis be put down to the impossibility of combining their conception of historical development as ruled by quasi-natural laws one the one hand with that of agents as the makers of their own history in any real sense on the other in a logically consistent way. The formula one may quote from their writings which is closest to a consistent answer to the riddle is probably that found in the Preface to the first volume of *Capital*:

> Even when a society has got on the scent of the natural law of its motion [*dem Naturgesetz ihrer Bewegung*] – and the ultimate purpose of this work is to disclose the economic law of motion [*das ökonomische Bewegungsgesetz*] of modern society – it can neither skip natural phases of development [*naturgemäße Entwicklungsphasen*] nor abolish them by decree. But it can shorten and alleviate the birthpangs.[230]

In other words, insofar as human actors are aware of the natural law of social development, they may shorten and alleviate the birthpangs by adapting their actions to it; but still, this does not make them the makers of their own history (under given circumstances) in any real sense rather than being the – in this case knowing and willing – bearers or supports of this law. And the ambiguity on this point of Marx' and Engels' various utterances about the motive power(s) of historical development is not eliminated by Marx' words a few pages earlier that,

---

[230] Marx, *Das Kapital*, 1, p. 15-16.

In itself, it is not a matter of the higher or lower degree of development of the social antagonisms which originate from the natural laws of capitalist production. It is a matter of these laws themselves, of these tendencies which have their effect and work themselves through with iron necessity. The more industrially developed country only shows the less developed one the picture of its own future.[231]

If no room is left for human agency to make *any* real difference at all in terms of the course of history, the analysis of the natural/economic law of motion of capitalist society and endeavours to organise the proletariat for its revolutionary historical role is irrelevant. If human agency can make a difference in terms of shortening and alleviating the birthpangs of historical development and transformations which will take place in any case, the knowledge of the inevitability of the process will be beneficial, but human agents are still not the makers of their own history, as they can only make it run its course faster and with less human suffering, not change it.

If, on the other hand, human agency can make a *real* difference to the actual *course* of historical development, what guarantee is there that the proletariat cannot fail to accomplish the transition to socialism and eventually classless communist society, given that the inevitability of that transition due to laws of historical development ruling the will, consciousness and intentions of agents is not, and cannot be, more than a hypothesis? And if such laws do rule the will, consciousness and intentions of agents, how can agents become aware (or remain unaware) of their interests in a socialist revolution or accomplish it (or fail to accomplish it) except through the

---

[231] Marx, *Das Kapital*, 1, p. 12.

effects of these laws? The tension in Marx' and Engels' historical materialism remains.

In fact, no less than four different conceptions of the degree to which human agents' will, consciousness and intentions are effective or ineffective in terms of the determination of historical development can be read from Marx' and Engels' mature texts:

1. Human agents make their own history, but not of their own free will, but under the given and inherited circumstances with which they are directly confronted, and with the tradition of the dead generations weighing like a nightmare on their minds.
2. History is ruled by iron-hard (quasi-)natural laws of development, but human agents may shorten and alleviate the birthpangs of historical transformations.
3. Human wills cancel out and thus allow (quasi-)natural laws to rule historical development.
4. Human will, consciousness and intentions are determined by the laws ruling the (quasi-)natural process of historical development.

The claims, in *The Communist Manifesto*,[232] *Capital* and *Anti-Dühring*, that the working class will inevitably respond, and respond successfully, to its plight in capitalism by effecting the transition from capitalism to socialism and eventually classless communist society, having been disciplined, united and organised "by the very mechanism of the process of capitalism itself",[233] may seem more plausible considered as an empirical hypothesis about the development of capitalism

---

[232] Marx & Engels, *Manifest der Kommunistischen Partei*, p. 474.
[233] Marx, *Das Kapital*, 1, p. 790-791. Engels, *Anti-Dühring*, p. 160 (*MEW*, 20, p. 124); cf. p. 332 (*MEW*, 20, p. 261), and Part III, ch. II, passim.

and working-class responses to it, responses that may be furthered by revolutionary theory, agitation and organisation. But firstly, they have not been confirmed by the historical development of capitalist societies so far; and secondly, they are made in the context of the very conception of the dialectic of forces and relations of production as the motive power of historical development and transformations.

Furthermore, this context strongly suggests that the first of the abovementioned four different conceptions of the degree to which human agents' will, consciousness and intentions are effective or ineffective in terms of the determination of historical development is in effect a foreign body in Marx' and Engels' mature conception of historical development and transformations, which is more consistent with the three other conceptions of the effectiveness or ineffectiveness of human agent's will, consciousness and intentions. Interpreters of Marx and Engels may advocate either of these three conceptions as the true Marx-Engelsian one by quoting the suitable passage or passages in the textual corpus, but objectively such cherry-picking must be considered futile. Both the irreducible presence of different conceptions concerning human wills, consciousness and intentions *and* the irreducible determinism, and tension, in Marx' and Engels' historical materialism can be established from their texts.

The logic of the notion of historical development as a process ruled by laws comparable to those ruling natural development, and of the conception of the dialectic of forces and relations of production as the motive power of historical development and transformations which is a more specific expression of that notion, tell against the conception of human agents as the makers of their own history and tend towards the conception of them as "only the *supports* or bearers of the guises (*Charaktermasken*) assigned to them by the structure of relations in the mode of production in the social formation", as it is expressed in Ben Brewster's Glossary to Althusser and Balibar. The claim that, "Hence each articulation of the mode of production and each level of the social formation defines for itself a potentially different form of historical individuality. The correspondence or non-correspondence of these forms of historical individuality plays an important part in transition"[234] may be read as an indication of the tension in the historical materialism which remains, and is, if anything, intensified, in this interpretation of it, part of which was Althusser's statement about the different forms of individuality required and produced by the capitalist mode of production, "of which the individuals are 'supports' (*Träger*), in the division of labour, in the different 'levels' of the structure".[235]

This reduction of agents to the mere bearers or supports of the character masks which their positions in the relations of production force on them, understood on functionalist assumptions, implied that the given type of society will reproduce itself endlessly; hence the rupture between abstract theory on the one hand and actual history on the other which eventually was made overt by Balibar's claim that, "the only real historical dialectic is the process of transformation of *each* concrete 'social formation' [.....] in reality they are the *only* object that is transformed, because they are the only one that really contains a history of class struggles."[236] This dead end of Althusserian structuralism has been dealt with elsewhere[237] and need not be further discussed here. It should only be emphasised that Marx and Engels never took their reflections on historical laws and human agency to the extreme found in Althusser & Balibar, and that the separation between self-reproducing modes of production on the one hand and

---

[234] Althusser & Balibar, p. 320.
[235] Althusser & Balibar, p. 112; cf. p. 180.
[236] Balibar, "Self Criticism", p. 59-60. Cf. Althusser & Balibar, p. 292-293.
[237] Gram-Jensen, *Structure, Agency and Theory*, Part One, ch. 1, b-c.

transformed concrete social formations on the other does not follow from the conception of the dialectic of forces and relations of production as the motive power of historical development and transformations found in Marx and Engels.

Admittedly, the agents constituting the class with an interest in the continued development of the productive forces fettered by the relations of production can be said to pursue their own ends when accomplishing a historical transformation. But if their doing so and their success in the endeavour are guaranteed by laws of historical development and transformations determining the will, consciousness and intentions of human agents, these same agents are *in effect* reduced to the supports or bearers of those laws. In other words, the idea that the transition from capitalism to socialism and eventually classless communist society is inevitable because of the laws ruling historical development renders the tension in Marx' and Engels' historical materialism ineradicable.

There can be no doubt about the theoretical *and* strategic implications of abandoning this idea, the conception of the dialectic of forces and relation of production as the motive power of historical development and transformations and Marx' confidence that,

> [.....]. No social order is ever destroyed before all the productive forces for which it is sufficient have been developed, and new superior relations of production never replace older ones before the material conditions for their existence have matured within the framework of the old society. Mankind thus inevitably sets itself only such tasks as it is able to solve, since closer examination will always show that the problem itself arises only when the material conditions for its

solution are already present or at least in the course of formation."[238]

Revolutionary-socialist strategy must be founded on the assumption that no such confidence is realistic, and that the accomplishment of the transition from capitalism to socialism and eventually classless communist society will, if it is feasible at all, depend on the right choices and actions being made by the socialist-revolutionary movement, that we cannot be sure that this will indeed be the case, and that the elimination of class divisions and exploitation will depend on the establishment of the *effectively* collective command of the means, process and outcome of production, which in its turn requires the establishment of *real and effective* democracy, in which decisions of any general importance about social development and conditions are *actually* made by the population itself.

The final goal is still the same: classless communist society defined by the collective command of the means, process and outcome of production. The abandonment of the confidence that it will inevitably be accomplished is the price paid for arriving at a realistic assessment of the problems involved in accomplishing it. If history is an open-ended process in which human agency may make the difference between the maintenance of capitalism and the transition to socialism and eventually classless communist society, there can be no guarantee that this transition will actually be accomplished, or that the abolition of capitalist relations of production will inevitably result in the transition to classless communist society rather than to new class divisions and forms of exploitation. And therefore, it is also necessary to secure the possibility of correcting or abandoning the very process of transition if it

---

[238] Marx, *A Contribution to the Critique of Political Economy*, p. 21 (*MEW*, 13, p. 9).

becomes clear that the latter rather than the former is going to eventuate from it.

Hopefully, the point that both a socialist and a classless communist society has to be *effectively ruled by its population*, to be an *effective* democracy in the full sense of that word, is no longer controversial. The reason why such societies have to be such genuine democracies follows from the very concept of communism as,

> a **mode of production** defined by the collective command of the means, process and outcome of production. *Collective* command is taken to imply both *common* and *equal* command. In other words, formal common ownership of means of production which are actually controlled by a minority of agents does *not* constitute communism. Such truly collective command requires free access to relevant information, and the freedom of expression, argument and decision for *all* (adult) members of society, with the corresponding institutional framework for democratic decision-making.[239]

Apart from the interest of agents in living in a society ruled by law, and in avoiding exploitation, the effective collective command of the means, process and outcome of production maximises their capacity to act, thus shaping their own life and the development of society to the highest possible degree.[240] This implies that:

1. The *effectively* collective command of the means, process and outcome of production which renders communist society classless, cannot be accomplished except in an effectively democratic framework.

---

[239] Gram-Jensen, *Structure, Agency and Theory*, p. 1328.
[240] Cf. Wright, *Classes*, p. 28, p. 36.

2.   If the effectively collective command of the means, process and outcome of production is not accomplished, the agents actually exercising that command will in effect constitute a new class able to exploit the rest of the population by virtue of their command of the means, process and outcome of production.

3.   Unless socialist society, the transitional phase between capitalist and classless communist society, realises effective democracy, the transition to classless communist society defined by the collective command of the means, process and outcome of production is thus unlikely to be accomplished.[241] The dictatorship of the proletariat, therefore, "can only have its proletarian class content by virtue of being democratic enough to allow that transition to classless communist society defined by the collective command of the means, process and outcome of production which is the fundamental class interest of the **working class**."[242]

As we know only too well from historical experience, a bourgeois society can dispense with democracy and civil freedoms and remain a bourgeois society; whereas a socialist or communist society cannot dispense with them without changing their very nature – that is, without ceasing to be a socialist or communist society.[243]

---

[241] "**Socialism**: transitional **mode of production**, the stage of transition, with a corresponding **type of society** and **type of state**, between capitalism and **communism**. A socialist society in the proper sense of the word will thus have the qualities required for the transition from capitalism into communism." (Gram-Jensen, *Structure, Agency and Theory*, p. 1334).

[242] Gram-Jensen, *Structure, Agency and Theory*, p. 1329; consequently, the term "dictatorship" refers *only*, in Marx' usage, to the class content of the state, not to its institutional organisation (p. 1328).

[243] Cf. Gram-Jensen, *Structure, Agency and Theory*, p. 900-901.

It should, then, go without saying that the realisation of a classless communist society implies a socialist *and* a communist state which is under real and firm democratic control, and that the freedom of organisation, expression and criticism, as well as rule by law, must be widened rather than restricted. While the socialist state must defend this revolutionary democracy against resistance to the process of transition by undemocratic means, whether from within or without the social formation(s) in question, and defend it effectively, it must never be allowed to render democracy ineffective, thus turning itself into a means of oppression of the majority and concentrating the command of the means, process and outcome of production in the hands of those in command of the state apparatus, thus turning them into a new exploiting class.

Here, one may acknowledge that Marx (and Engels) were firmly committed to the idea of *the working class*, not a revolutionary *party*, as the revolutionary subject,[244] and obviously envisaged a democratic rule not *for*, but *by* the people in post-revolution society.[245] Marx' vision and expectations were condensed in his words written in 1852,[246] addressed to the workers that, "You will have to go through 15, 20, 50 years of civil wars and popular struggles, not just to change conditions but to change yourselves and grow capable of political rule".[247] In a circular letter of 17/18 September 1879, he and Engels confirmed their conviction that the liberation of the working class has to be the work of the working class itself, as written by Marx in the provisional statutes of the

---

[244] Marx, "Inauguraladresse der Internationalen Arbeiter-Assoziation", p. 12-13. Cf. Marx & Engels, *Manifest der Kommunistischen Partei*, p. 472-474. Marx, *Das Kapital*, 1, p. 790-791.

[245] Marx, *Der Bürgerkrieg in Frankreich*, p. 338-340.

[246] *MEW*, 8, p. 406.

[247] Marx, *Enthüllungen über den Kommunisten-Prozeß zu Köln*, p. 412.

International Workers' Association in 1864,[248] adding that they could thus not unite with people claiming that the workers are too uneducated to liberate themselves and must be liberated from above, by philanthropic members of big and petty bourgeoisie.[249]

It is not too much to say that in the *Manifesto*, the Preface to *A Contribution to the Critique of Political Economy*, *Capital* and *Anti-Dühring*, central texts as far as Marx' and Engels' statements on their historical materialism *and* their expectations about and confidence in the transition from capitalism to socialism and eventually classless communist society are concerned, their expectations and confidence are based on the conception of the dialectic of forces and relations of production as the motive power of historical development and transformations, and on that of history in general and the development of capitalism in particular as ruled by quasi-natural *laws* – although human agency (including the expectation that the growth, discipline, unity and organisation of the working class will be furthered by the very mechanism of capitalist production itself[250]), and human agents as the makers of their own history,[251] are also present.

As obvious from later historiography, working-class (and other class) responses to the developments of capitalism in general and the modern history of advanced capitalist

---

[248] Marx, "Provisorische Statuten der Internationalen Arbeiter-Assoziation", p. 14.
[249] Marx & Engels, ["Zirkularbrief an Bebel, Liebknecht, Bracke u.a."], p. 165.
[250] Marx, *Das Kapital*, 1, p. 790-791. Cf. Engels, *Anti-Dühring*, p. 160 (*MEW*, 20, p. 124).
[251] And, in late letters from Engels, the irreducibility of concrete history ("Engels an Conrad Schmidt, 5. August 1890"; "Engels an Conrad Schmidt, 27. Oktober 1890"; "Engels an Joseph Bloch in Königsberg, 21./22. September 1890").

societies in particular have made a difference to this very development – in *other* ways than effecting a transition to socialism and eventually (or more modestly: towards) classless communist society. Working-class organisation and class struggle there have been, but also working-class *dis*organisation and isolation of class struggle, as well as the trajectory of the rise, development and fall of "real existing socialism".

As a kind of parenthesis, a few remarks on the question of whether human consciousness, and hence the will and intentions, of human agents are strictly determined or at least to some extent free from (pre)determination may be inserted here.

Writing that, "Human societies secrete ideology as the very element and atmosphere indispensable to their historical respiration and life",[252] about the capitalist mode producing the different forms of individuality it requires[253] and that, "Precisely because it is determined by its structure, at the level of experience the social whole remains *opaque* to the agents",[254] Althusser and Poulantzas seem to overlook the fact that if their assertions are true, they themselves must be subjected to the same secretion of ideology, formation of their individuality and inability to recognise the social whole for what it is – that is, that they must themselves be assumed to suffer from and produce ideological illusions rather than (valid) theory or knowledge.

And something similar may be said about Marx' approval of the Russian reviewer's words about laws (specific to the individual historical periods) ruling the will, consciousness and intentions of agents: if so, what difference can theoretical

---

[252] Althusser, *For Marx*, p. 232.
[253] Althusser & Balibar, p. 112.
[254] Poulantzas, p. 207.

efforts make, and how can the truth or falsehood of the outcome of these efforts be meaningfully assessed if our will, consciousness and intentions are determined by laws of social development in this way? Theorists should never forget that they, too, are agents subjected to the same conditions for observation as everyone else, even if their observations are made in a more systematic way than those of others. The quotation above from Marx' Afterword to the 2nd edition of *Capital*[255] should suffice to indicate the consequent problem with that text.

The quotation, which is obviously rather similar to (but not identical with) Engels' later argument on agents' wills cancelling out, thus allowing history to proceed in the manner of a natural process and essentially subject to the same laws of motion,[256] should be interpreted with some care. In the first place, it is after all written by somebody else, who may not have meant exactly with these words what Marx took them to mean. And secondly, the way Marx and Engels kept expounding the relationship between agency on the one hand and laws of social/historical development on the other may suggest that they were never really able to find a formula which they found wholly satisfactory.

All the same, Marx obviously had no issue with the reviewer's words about "the social movement" as "a process of natural history ruled by laws that are not only independent of the will, consciousness and intentions of people, but on the contrary determine their will, consciousness and intentions", and about "the specific laws ruling the origin, existence, development, death of a given social organism and its substitution by another, higher one" obviously reading the latter as referring

---

[255] Marx, *Das Kapital*, 1, p. 25-27.
[256] Engels, "Engels an Joseph Bloch in Königsberg, 21./22. September 1890", p. 464.

to the conception of the dialectic of forces and relations of production as the motive power of historical development and transformations which informed ch. 24.7 of *Capital* on the historical tendency of capitalist accumulation. As the words stand, they suggest a problem similar to that with Althusser's and Poulantzas' idea about ideology being imposed on agents' minds by a process which may certainly be considered "ruled by laws that are not only independent of the will, consciousness and intentions of people, but on the contrary determine their will, consciousness and intentions."[257]

If such laws ruling historical development determine our will, consciousness and intentions, then any ideas we have about social reality and how we should respond to it must be so determined, by processes independent of agency and determining the will, consciousness and intentions of social analysts no less than those of other agents. If so, how can we assess the truth of what we think we know? And if we *can* argue rationally about social reality, does this not mean that we can modify our consciousness by this process, so that our acquisition of true knowledge makes, or may make, a real difference to future developments? And does the possibility of acquiring true knowledge not require some degree of freedom to change our minds, and test theories, by means of logical argument and evidence – that is, some freedom from laws determining our consciousness, and hence also our will and intentions? So that the lack of any such freedom implies the futility of arguing in terms of logic and evidence? As Grue-Sørensen argued against the idea of strict determination of our thoughts, which in effect reduces "thinking" to an involuntary process like sweating on a hot day, "according to this view our thinking is determined in one context, the causal one, to such a degree that no mobility remains in the other, the logical one; and all our thinking and arguing against each

---

[257] Marx, *Das Kapital*, 1, p. 26-27.

other presupposes this mobility in consideration of correctness."[258] In other words, if our consciousness is lawed in the sense suggested by the Russian reviewer, historical *knowledge* or any conception of the process of historical development is also so determined, and hence impossible to assess in terms of truth or falsehood – which, if so, also goes for the assumption that it *is* lawed in this sense, this assumption consequently being self-defeating, and implying the reduction of any theories and ideas about social – indeed any – reality to the same indeterminable status. To offer a concrete example, Wright has written that,

> [.....]. Class interests in capitalist society are those potential objectives which become actual objectives of struggle in the absence of the mystifications and distortions of capitalist relations. Class interests, therefore, are in a sense hypotheses: they are hypotheses about the objectives of struggles which would occur if the actors in the struggle had a scientifically correct understanding of their situations.[259]

However, if our consciousness is lawed in the suggested sense, the making of and argument about such hypotheses is meaningless, because it is impossible to distinguish a scientifically correct understanding of our situations from mystifications and distortions by means of any rational argument, as the very idea of rational argument is meaningless if our thinking is reducible to an involuntary process occurring in our brains like the process of digestion in our bowels. As Favrholdt observed, "we have to assume that our thinking is to some extent not determined if we are to be able to use the

---

[258] Knud Grue-Sørensen, *Studier over refleksivitet*, J. H. Schultz Forlag, København 1950, p. 191, quoted from Favrholdt, p. 283.
[259] Wright, *Class, Crisis and the State*, p. 89.

concepts "truth", "falsity" and "meaning" in an understandable way."[260]

More specifically, a logical implication of the positing of laws determining the consciousness, will and intentions of agents is that Marx' and Engels' consciousness, will and intentions are also determined by these laws, which excludes any rational discussion about the reality or otherwise of them, indeed that any theoretical argument in a meaningful sense is both meaningless and irrelevant, as the articulation of agents' consciousness and the quasi-natural process of historical development will proceed as determined by the laws ruling them anyway. Judging from what else Marx and Engels wrote, it is improbable that they would accept this implication of their preoccupation with laws of historical development, and thus a fair guess that they would have been ready to modify the view described by the Russian reviewer if they had been confronted with that implication.[261] But the reality of the tension in their historical materialism is certainly demonstrated by Marx' endorsement of the reviewer's words.

It might be argued that the German *bestimmen* in the quotation above from the Afterword should be understood as "determine" in the Wrightean sense of delimiting a field of the possible with pressures and probabilities leaving room for agency to make a difference.[262] But then how can the process of

---

[260] Favrholdt, p. 283; cf. p. 159.

[261] In any case this view seems incompatible with their rejection of the idea that history – as if it were a person apart – uses man as a means of going through with *its* ends and their insistence that history "is *nothing* but the activity of man pursuing his own ends" (Marx & Engels, *Die heilige Familie*, p. 98; cf. *Die deutsche Ideologie*, p. 45).

[262] As the word may, and probably should, be read in the passage in the 1859 Preface stating that, "It is not the consciousness of men that determines their existence, but their social existence that

historical development be a process of natural history ruled by laws which are not only independent of the will, consciousness and intentions of agents, but on the contrary determine them, rule [*lenken*] them? What then has become of history being nothing but agents pursuing their *own* ends? Human beings making their life activity an object of their will and consciousness, able to contemplate themselves in a world they have themselves created?[263] These same human beings as the makers of their own history? Or the historical and moral element involved in the determination of the value of labour-power?[264] The tension, and the ambiguity or vacillation in the conception of the nature of the process of historical development, remain.

So, what is the conclusion? No absolutely unequivocal conclusion about Marx' and Engels' thoughts about agency and laws and the relationship between them in the determination of historical development can be offered, precisely because of this ineradicable tension, with the consequent ambiguity or vacillation, in what they wrote about this subject. The formulations in their texts cannot be summarised in any single unequivocal formula consistent with all of them and their implications. It may, however, as a tentative summary be stated that some causal effectiveness is allowed to agency in their concrete analyses[265] as well as the formulations in *Die heilige Familie* and *Die deutsche Ideologie* cited above, while the conception of the dialectic of forces and relations of production as

---

determines their consciousness [*Es ist nicht das Bewußtsein der Menschen, das ihr Sein, sondern umgekehrt ihr gesellschaftliches Sein, das ihr Bewußtsein bestimmt*]." (Marx, *A Contribution to the Critique of Political Economy*, p. 21 (*MEW*, 13, p. 9)).

[263] Marx, *Early Writings*, p. 328-329 (*MEW*, Ergänzungsband, erster Teil, p. 516-517).

[264] Marx, *Das Kapital*, 1, p. 185.

[265] E. g. Marx, *The Class Struggles in France*, *The Eighteenth Brumaire of Louis Bonaparte*, and *Capital*, 1, ch. 8, sections 5-7.

the motive power of historical development and transformations tended to dominate their forecasts and general statements on the transition from capitalism to socialism and eventually classless communist society; and that one finds a perhaps increasing tendency in their writings to emphasise *laws* of historical development. What can be said with certainty on the basis of Marx' and Engels' writings is, however, that since the mid-1840s they considered the transition from capitalism to socialism and eventually classless communist society inevitable, and that their expectations and predictions to this effect were based on their conception of the dialectic of forces and relations of production as the motive power of historical development and transformations. And that they consequently did not consider the potential of agency to make a real difference to the course of historical development large enough to be decisive in this regard. Again, their expectations and predictions have not, so far, been confirmed by the historical record.

The conception of determination (in the last instance) as the delimitation of a field of the possible with pressures and probabilities within which social circumstances and agency interact makes it possible to think of agency as determined in the last instance by social circumstances with the mode and relations of production at their core, but still as a co-determinant of actual historical development and transformations, a co-determinant irreducible to the effects of quasi-natural laws of historical development. The argument against Marx' and Engels' expectations and predictions rests on the assumption that agents have to find out about their situation and possibilities ("who are we, what is our situation, and what can and should be done about it?") and try to act on what they find out, by means of whatever capacities they have.[266]

---

[266] This raises the question of *class capacities*, "class capacities for struggle" being defined as "the organizational, ideological and

162

Again, Marx and Engels expected working-class capacities to be augmented by capitalism itself, so that the working class would be capable to accomplish the transition to socialism and eventually classless communist society once the concentration of capital and the socialisation of labour had at last reached a point where they became incompatible with their capitalist integument, which would consequently be burst asunder.[267] But this has not been confirmed by the history of advanced capitalist societies, where class struggle has generally been limited to such forms as do not objectively threaten to disrupt the capitalist type of society and the dominant relations of production.

Apart from repression, major causes of this have been various compromises with immediate political and economic working-class interests as well as the establishment of hierarchies in terms of income, conditions of work and status within the working class and the consequent competition between various parts and individual members of the class for (monopoly of) positions in such hierarchies, along with the negative example of post-1917 "real existing socialism".[268]

In *A Revised Historical Materialism*, the idea of collective subjects is rejected.[269] Agents (individuals) may organise or be

---

material resources available to class agents" (Wright, Levine & Sober, p. 29).

[267] Marx, *Das Kapital*, 1, p. 790-791. Engels, *Anti-Dühring*, p. 159-160; cf. Part III, ch. II.

[268] Cf. Gram-Jensen, *Structure, Theory and Agency*, Part Three, ch. 1; the above is a mere adumbration.

[269] Gram-Jensen, *A Revised Historical Materialism*, p. 11; cf. *Structure, Agency and Theory*, p. 1327: an *actor* is defined as "either an individual (agent) performing some action or an organisation which coordinates the actions of individuals into collective practice, i. e. a

organised as collective *actors*, e. g. political parties, trade unions or other interest organisations, governments, a board of directors, etcetera, etcetera, etcetera. But such actors are not *subjects* in the same sense as the individual agents which are members of them and produce their activity by interacting with each other. That is, the collective actor does not have any will, consciousness or intentions of its own apart from the irreducibly individual wills, consciousnesses and intentions of these interacting agents, although the interaction is structured and directed by various goals, rules, norms and habits of the institution etcetera in question, as well as its resources, social context and concrete situation. The individual wills, consciousnesses and intentions of their members will enter into the process of shaping the activities of the collective actors, e. g. by individual capacities or shortcomings, experiences, opinions, ambitions and sympathies or antipathies influencing their decisions and the ways in which they cooperate or fail to cooperate.

The other side of this conceptualisation is that the mere sharing of social positions and/or functions, or conditions, or other characteristics, does *not* turn a group of individual agents into a collective actor: this takes *organisation*, the establishment of a framework for the interaction of a more or less regular kind for various purposes between these agents, their cooperation for a specific occasion or more permanently. Hence a social *class* as such is not in itself an actor or a subject. Whereas members of a class (or of several classes) may for some occasion or more permanently form a collective actor by organised cooperation serving some purpose.

Why is this important? In the first place it is important because the reduction of agents' will, consciousness and

---

practice different from their mere sum total"; an *agent* as "an individual human being in its capacity as actor".

intentions to forms of individuality or ideology imposed on them by the capitalist mode of production or by capitalist society, or for that matter by laws ruling historical development and transformations,[270] hardly makes it possible to account cogently for the history of that society. And secondly, it is important because it emphasises the open-endedness of the process of historical development of which agents' articulation of their experiences of and responses to their "lived" reality is an irreducible, inevitable and, within the limits set by what is there to experience and respond to, *unpredictable* part. Or more precisely, it is structurally determined, but cannot, as such, be taken to be limited to only one possible course of development. Hence "the development of consciousness and agency leading towards socialist revolution"[271] cannot be taken for granted.

Popper's observation of the fact that we cannot predict the future growth of our scientific knowledge, and hence not the future course of human history, and more generally that, *"if there is such a thing as growing human knowledge, then we cannot anticipate today what we shall know only tomorrow"*,[272] was quoted in *A Revised Historical Materialism*,[273] and the point hardly needs to be further elaborated. The fact that human beings relate consciously to their given circumstances and hence make their own social history under these same given and inherited circumstances means that unless human beings' responses are predictable, the future development of this social history is not predictable either; and in addition one may add that human beings' metabolism with nature on which their existence

---

[270] Althusser, *For Marx*, p. 232. Althusser & Balibar, p. 110-111. Poulantzas, p. 207. Marx, *Das Kapital*, 1, p. 25-27.

[271] Gram-Jensen, *Structure, Agency and Theory*, p. 22; quotation from anonymous reader's report, private communication to this writer from Dr. David Laibman, 20 August, 2007.

[272] Popper, *The Poverty of Historicism*, p. vi-vii.

[273] Gram-Jensen, *A Revised Historical Materialism*, p. 57-58.

is based, and nature's effect on their existence generally, may also confront them with circumstances, such as climatic changes or epidemics the nature and effects of which cannot be precisely predicted either. Hence the question of how to accomplish a transition from capitalism to socialism and eventually classless communist society is not merely one of how to shorten and alleviate the birthpangs most effectively.

Marx' acceptance of the Russian reviewer's description of the dialectical method involving the assumption that laws ruling historical development determine human beings' will, consciousness and intentions and Engels' conception of parallelograms of forces may be considered two ways of arguing why the future development of social history *is* indeed predictable. Marx was certainly not unaware of "false consciousness" and wrong responses of workers to their "lived" reality, such as the competition between English and Irish workers, reformism or workers' chauvinism;[274] but judging from the evidence, he does not seem to have been overly worried about them as far as the long perspective was concerned – logically enough on the assumption that the laws of history guarantee a transition from capitalism to socialism and eventually classless communist society. And yet he criticised and warned against working-class chauvinism and urged workers not to fight only for reforms, but also for the abolition of capitalism.[275] So, while it is true that Marx accepted the Russian reviewer's description of the dialectical method, Sørensen is also right when he states that, "Marx and Engels consider workers' consciousness at any given moment the outcome of a struggle back and forth between opposite classes, groups

---

[274] Marx, "Der Generalrat an den Föderalrat der romanischen Schweiz", p. 388-389; *Lohn, Preis und Profit*, p.152; "Marx an Sigfried Meyer und August Vogt in New York, 9. April 1870", p. 668-669. Cf. Sørensen, *Marxismen og den sociale orden*, p. 502, and Mau, *Mute Compulsion*, p. 302.
[275] Marx, *Lohn, Preis und Profit*, p. 152.

and ideologies and not as any automatic reflexion of given socioeconomic positions."[276] Marx is quite obviously inconsistent on this point.

Likewise, in the second address of the General Council on the Franco-Prussian War, Marx wrote,

> May the sections of the *International Workers' Association* in all countries exhort the working class to active stirrings (*tätiger Bewegung*). If the workers forget their duty, if they remain passive, the present terrible war will be but the harbinger of still more terrible international fights, and will in every country lead to new defeats of the workman by the lords of the sword, of landed property and of capital.[277]

This warning is consistent enough with the idea of human beings as the makers of their own history whose responses make a difference, for better or worse, to the actual course of history, and for that matter with the idea of the working class being in due course "disciplined, united, organized by the very mechanism of the process of capitalist production itself"[278] – but not with the idea of their will, consciousness and intentions being determined by laws comparable to those ruling natural development,[279] or that of human actor's wills

---

[276] Sørensen, *Marxismen og den sociale orden*, p. 502; cf. *Den europæiske deltagelseskrise*, p. 70-71.

[277] Marx, *Zweite Adresse des Generalrats über den Deutsch-Französischen Krieg*, p. 278.

[278] Marx, *Das Kapital*, 1, p. 791. Cf. Engels, *Anti-Dühring*, p. 160 (*MEW*, 20, p. 124).

[279] On this assumption, one cannot say that history is *nothing* but the activities of human agents pursuing their own ends: it is rather the effects of the laws of historical development brought about by means of the activities of human agents determined by those laws,

cancelling out, thus allowing such quasi-natural laws to determine the course of historical development.

Geras has made the point that,

> [.....] Scientific knowledge *in its content* is universal and objective, not dependent for its *validity* on the values and perspectives of this social group or that historical epoch, not therefore merely a matter of opinion or of interest. By emphasising this, Althusser reasserts knowledge's rights against all forms of relativism, which, 'proving' in their theories of knowledge, of ideology and utopia, that all knowledge is necessarily partial and subjective, cannot escape the contradiction and embarrassment of claiming to be the knowledge of the impossibility of knowledge.[280]

The assertion that our knowledge (of social reality) is inevitably partial, approximate and provisional,[281] does not imply that it is subjective or invalid, merely that it cannot, firstly, be complete, that is, a final knowledge of everything pertaining to its object (social reality or something else, perhaps reality in general), and, secondly, that there is always the possibility that it must be revised at various points; this does not mean that no such thing as valid, objective knowledge (true about reality regardless of what we think, and of values, perspectives and interests) is feasible. Geras is, moreover, right in emphasising that scientific practice, the production of knowledge, is

---

as they determine the will, consciousness and intentions of those human agents.

[280] Geras, *Literature of Revolution*, p. 122; the passage should not be read to mean that Geras is not critical of Althusser's position on knowledge and science (ibid. and ff).

[281] Gram-Jensen, *A Revised Historical Materialism*, p. 17, p. 66; p. 209: "partial, approximate and subject to revision". Cf. Thompson, *The Poverty of Theory and Other Essays*, p. 39.

a social practice inevitably, like any other social practice, taking place on determinate (and more or less propitious) social conditions; and that the capitalist working class and its political practice were necessary preconditions for the elaboration of Marxist theory.[282] The obvious implication of this, in its turn, is that this theory must also be informed by subsequent historical development.

Post-Marxian experience (which is obviously not *final* either!) demonstrates the *incompleteness* of Marx' and Engels' (and e. g. Lenin's and Luxemburg's) experience on which (combined with their philosophical and social-theoretical heritage) their revolutionary optimism – *and* the conception of the dialectic of forces and relations of production as the motive power of historical development and transformations guaranteeing the transition from capitalism to socialism and eventually classless communist society – was based.

Obviously, historical experience and knowledge – whether about the past or the present – is the available source of information on which to build theories about the kind of process historical development is, what opportunities and hindrances the present conjuncture and near future offers, and how to handle them – but experience so far is inevitably never *final*, as *future* developments, which may give rise to intrinsically new conjunctures, opportunities, hindrances and, hence, intrinsically new experiences and knowledge, cannot be known or foreseen today.

History until now, including the present conjuncture, is all we have to build on and reason from, incomplete as the record is, and given the intrinsic limits to historical knowledge (knowledge which, *pace* Hindess & Hirst, may at least warn of the difficulties of predicting the future – as well as some of

---

[282] Geras, *Literature of Revolution*, p. 125-129.

the difficulties that may have to be faced, and some of the mistakes that have to be avoided). But we cannot do anything better than using what experiences and knowledge we have and learning from it to the best of our ability, and then proceed by trial, error and corrections.

Geras quoted Trotsky to the effect that,

> The identity, in principle, of the interests of the proletariat and of the aims of the ... party does not mean either that the proletariat as a whole is, even today, conscious of its class interests, or that the party under all conditions formulates them *correctly*. The very need of the party originates in the ... fact that the proletariat is not born with the innate understanding of its historical interests. The task of the party consists in *learning*, from experience derived from the struggle, how to demonstrate to the proletariat its right to leadership.

To which Geras added the comment that, "The emphasis here is as much on the need for the party to learn from the class by direct participation in the struggles of that class, as it is on its role as leader or educator. The possibility of a consciousness adequate to the task of overthrowing capitalism is thus made dependent on the mutual interaction between party and class."[283]

According to Marx' words in the 1859 Preface and in *Capital*,[284] his and Engels' words in the *Manifesto*, section I, and Engels' words in *Anti-Dühring*,[285] to mention just those

---

[283] Geras, *Literature of Revolution*, p. 174. Quotation from Trotsky, *Their Morals and Ours*, New York 1966, p. 38.
[284] Marx, *A Contribution to the Critique of Political Economy*, p. 21-22 (*MEW*, 13, p. 8-9); *Das Kapital*, 1, Preface to first edition, ch. 24.7).
[285] Engels, *Anti-Dühring*, p. 159-160, p. 188-189, (*MEW*, 20, p. 123-124, p. 146-147), Part III, ch. II, passim.

examples, the transition from capitalism to socialism and eventually classless communist society is possible, and thanks to the laws ruling historical developments and transformations, and capitalist development which will itself produce the required working-class capacities, the difference made by agents' understanding or lack of understanding of the said laws is reduced to that of succeeding or failing in shortening and alleviating the birthpangs.[286]

The development in Marx' and Engels' lifetimes, indeed the development up to the outbreak of the 1st World War, could in fact seemingly, although, as it turned out, erroneously, be interpreted as a confirmation of their expectations and predictions: the development of the productive forces, the growth of the working class and workers' organisations, including socialist parties and the First and Second Internationals, despite their theoretical and ideological shortcomings. That from the outbreak of the 1st World War and on certainly leaves room for less optimism.

It is, of course, possible to postulate that what we have seen is, after all, a number of temporary setbacks, and that it is all just because "the time line for the development of consciousness and agency leading toward socialist revolution has turned out to be longer than we had thought, and hoped for."[287] But considering, firstly, that the basis for Marx' and Engels' expectations and predictions is actually little if anything more than a *hypothesis* about the laws of historical development, more precisely the conception of the dialectic of forces and relations of production as the motive power of historical development and transformations, and, secondly,

---

[286] Marx, *Das Kapital*, 1, p. 15-16.
[287] Anonymous reader's report, private communication to this writer from Dr. David Laibman, quoted in Gram-Jensen, *Structure, Agency and Theory*, p. 22.

the post-1914 historical experiences, including the trajectory of post-1917 "real existing socialism", it seems somewhat overly sanguine to rely on such bland optimism. How is the isolation of class struggle to be broken? What, if any, *strategy* for the transition from capitalism to socialism and eventually classless communist society will be effective? How is a socialist, and eventually communist, society and production to be organised? Will they be able to function at the required level of *sustainable* material production? The temptation to leave the answer to the future is understandable on Marx' and Engels' assumptions and expectations, but the consequence is that we are left with a yawning strategic gap. As Anderson has argued,

> [.....]. The most hazardous conclusions that the system of *Capital* yielded were the general theorem of the falling rate of profit, and the tenet of an ever-increasing class polarization between bourgeoisie and proletariat. Neither has yet been adequately substantiated. The first implied an economic breakdown of capitalism by its inner mechanisms; the second a social breakdown by way – if not an immiseration of the proletariat – of an ultimate absolute preponderance of a vast industrial working class of productive labourers over a tiny bourgeoisie, with few or no intermediary groups. The very absence of any political theory proper in the late Marx may thus be logically related to a latent catastrophism in his economic theory, which rendered the development of the former redundant.[288]

As noted in *A Revised Historical Materialism*, the "catastrophism" is hardly latent, as the prediction of the inevitability of the fall of the bourgeoisie and the victory of the proletariat in *Capital* is most explicit and explicitly refers to that made in

---

[288] Anderson, *Considerations on Western Marxism*, p. 115-116.

the *Manifesto*, which is indeed quoted in a footnote.[289] But the real point is of course that the expectation that the transition from capitalism to socialism and eventually classless communist society is guaranteed by the laws ruling the process of historical development and transformations, and more specifically the dialectic of forces and relations of production assumed to be the motive power of this process, part of which was the working class being increased in numbers, disciplined, united and organised by the process of capitalist production itself, made a serious investigation into such factors as might counteract the supersession of capitalism by socialism and eventually communism, and the elaboration of a strategy for overcoming them, seem superfluous.

---

[289] Marx, *Das Kapital*, 1, p. 790-791.

9. The Need for a Revision.

The fundamental tension in Marx' and Engels' historical materialism on which the case for the revision of it to a large extent turns, is not that between the conception of the level of development of the productive forces determining social relations on the one hand and the conception of the social relations of production determining the structure of production "so that 'production corresponds to class antagonism'" on the other[290] argued by Rigby, real as that tension may be in itself:[291]

> The foundations of Marx's two theories of history should now be clear. In the first, based on the primacy of the productive forces, material production gives us social relations. In the second theory, production itself is seen as a social activity, structured by the distribution of the instruments of labour through specific relations of production such as the possession of tools by the medieval artisan, or the divorce of the wage labourer from the means of production under capitalism. [.....]. Marx's position remained inconsistent and ambiguous. He continued to assert the claims of productive force determinism even after formulating a concept of production as social production which provided an implicit critique of those claims.[292]

---

[290] Rigby, p. 149.

[291] Apart from the question of the textual evidence, which will not be entered into here, it may be a matter of looking at the interaction (and mutual setting of limits to the possible) between the level of development of the productive forces and the social relations of production from different angles. In any case, the question of the two theories Rigby ascribes to Marx is not central to that of determinism in Marx and Engels.

[292] Rigby, p. 148.

The fundamental tension is that between the conception of the dialectic of forces and relations of production as the motive power of historical development and transformations on the one hand and that of the interaction between social circumstances and agency – the conception of human beings as the makers of their own history under given conditions which implies that interaction as that motive power – on the other, which is thus also a tension between the conception of historical development and transformations as *lawed* on the one hand and the conception of it as *open-ended* (within limits) on the other. In any case, the following passage in *Capital* couples the specific form in which unpaid labour is extracted from the immediate producers with a specific corresponding level or stage of development [*Entwicklungsstufe*] of the mode of labour and hence the social power of production, and identifies the immediate relationship of the owners of the means of production [*Produktionsbedingungen*] to the immediate producers as "the innermost secret, the hidden basis of the whole social construction":

> The specific economic form in which unpaid surplus labour is pumped from the immediate producers determines the relationship between master and servant as it springs immediately from production itself and in its turn reacts on it as a determinant [*und seinerseits bestimmend auf sie zurückwirkt*]. But on this the whole formation of the economic community [*Gemeinwesen*] which springs from the relations of production themselves, and thus at the same time its specific political form, is based. It is every time the immediate relationship of the owners of the means of production to the immediate producers – a relationship the current form of which always quite naturally corresponds to a specific stage of development of the mode of labour and thus its social power of production – in which we find

the innermost secret, the hidden basis of the whole social construction and hence also the political form of
the relations of sovereignty and dependence, in brief
the current specific form of the state. This does not
mean that the same economic basis – the same in
terms of the main conditions – cannot, due to countless different empirical circumstances, natural conditions, race relations, external historical influences etcetera, exhibit endless variations and shades which can
only be understood by analysing these empirically
given circumstances.[293]

It may well be a real merit of the conception of the interaction
between social circumstances and agency as the motive
power of historical development and transformations that it
does not suggest any specific mechanism of transition from
one mode of production and type of society to another. In
contradistinction to the conception of the dialectic of forces
and relations of production as the motive power of historical
development and transformations, this leaves the field open
for a variety of actual causes of actual transitions to be established by historical analysis, and perhaps by future experience,
something which will of course contribute to the understanding of the nature of the interaction between social circumstances and agency itself.

Marx and Engels kept oscillating, as it were, between activist
politics and a theory of history which is both explicitly and
implicitly determinist in the sense of meaning that the transition from capitalism to socialism and eventually classless
communist society is inevitable, because history is ruled by
quasi-natural laws, never really establishing a credible basis
for their unification. Marx' quotation from the Russian reviewer in the Preface to the 2nd edition of *Capital* and Engels'

---

[293] Marx, *Das Kapital*, 3, p. 799-800.

hypothesis on the parallelograms of forces and human wills cancelling out, thus allowing those quasi-natural laws to work, their conception of the dialectic of forces and relations of production as the motive power of historical development and transformations and their predictions about the inevitability of the said transition represent the determinist pole. Their work to further the organisation and revolutionary consciousness of the working class and their emphasis on human beings as the makers of their own history[294] represent the other, activist one.

The tension between Marx' quotation from the Russian reviewer and Engels' argument on the parallelograms of power on the one hand and the passages in their works emphasising agents, human beings, as the makers of their own history (on given conditions), a history consisting of human agents' pursuit of their own ends,[295] on the other is real. *It cannot be both ways*: human beings making their own history *and* their will, consciousness and intentions determined by laws ruling historical development (*or* their wills (and consciousness and intentions) cancelling out, leaving quasi-natural laws to rule historical development).

To explain why the experiences and responses of a particular group of agents at a specific point in time and space were

---

[294] To avoid any misunderstandings: it is not part of the critique of Marx and Engels that they ever made any assertion to the effect that human beings make their own history *as they please*, let alone that they *should* have made such assertions; this writer fully agrees with Marx' statement that human beings make their own history under the given and inherited circumstances with which they are directly confronted (Marx, *The Eighteenth Brumaire of Louis Bonaparte*, p. 146 (*MEW*, 8, p. 115). Historical development establishes the conditions on which the interaction between social circumstances and agency takes place.
[295] Marx & Engels, *Die heilige Familie*, p. 98.

articulated in the way they were (itself something to be read from historical evidence), it is necessary to ascertain as precisely as possible what the world, the society of which they were part and their own specific place and situation in it looked like to them; what traditions of the dead generations weighed like a nightmare on their minds, what alternative ideologies were articulated by other groups, the distribution of ideological and other resources, whatever ongoing struggles and conflicts, wars etcetera which were parts of their "lived" reality and how all this (and more?) was reflected in the minds of members of the group, readable from their utterances and actions insofar as it is ascertainable from the relevant sources.

Comparative studies may identify similar ideological forms in particular types of society, suggesting their common traits as causal factors; and divergent forms which must be accounted for by specific traits and processes. Broadly speaking, it seems safe to say that similar conditions tend towards similarity, different ones towards differences, which is hardly surprising but suggests the limits set by social structure *and* the causal efficacy of concrete circumstances within this delimitation of the field(s) of the possible. At the same time, responses in one social formation, or responses of some groups in the same social formation, may inspire others, but it must be assumed that they only do so insofar as they seem to *make sense of* agents' situations.

These considerations also suggest, once again, why the relationship between structural and historical analysis is one of *complementarity*: both are irreducible to the other, and the logic of the structure (the (dominant) mode of production, the type of society) is tempered by agency as well as setting limits to the possible, agents realising some possibilities rather than others in a process in which concrete circumstances, choices and actions cannot be abstracted from.

Thus, for example, party systems develop on the basis of social classes, interests, responses and conflicts, but also according to the precise forms of political institutions and the *concrete* course of events, nationally and internationally. There is not *one* capitalist form of regime, functionally adapted to the type of society, but state apparatuses and regimes formed and reformed through the actual course of historical development. In the analysis of actual historical development, the difference made by what we *think* about the world and our possibilities, that is, by our concrete articulation of our experiences of and responses to our "lived" reality, cannot be abstracted from. Nor, on the other hand, does the real effect of our consciousness on our actions render the objective facts about the world and our possibilities null and void: it is the *interaction* between human agency: our responses to our "lived" reality based on the experiences of it we articulate, on the one hand and the objective nature of the reality we try to handle on the other which constitutes the process of history.

Engels' idea of historical development arising from conflicts between many individual wills and thus resulting from "an infinite series of parallelograms of forces", so that it is "the product of a power which works as a whole *unconsciously* and without volition"[296] is an unavailing attempt to overcome the tension between the idea of human agents as the makers of their own history (on given and inherited circumstances and with the tradition of the dead generations weighing like a nightmare on their minds) on the one hand and that of history as a process ruled by laws comparable to those ruling natural processes on the other. It is unavailing because the pull and push of conflicting wills cannot be assumed to *cancel out* and thus render the actual effect on social development of

---

[296] Engels, "Engels an Joseph Bloch in Königsberg, 21./22. September 1890", p. 464.

what ends agents pursue, and thus of the content and relative strengths of their wills, null and void, and the process of social development hence comparable to natural processes,[297] even if it is still true that history "is *nothing* but the activity of man pursuing his own ends."[298]

Engels' idea of parallelograms of forces must indeed be considered a kind of antithesis to the definition of history as *nothing* but the activity of human beings pursuing their own ends – the reduction of this activity to a mere tool or vehicle for the quasi-natural laws supposed to rule the process of historical development in the same way in which natural laws rule that of natural development. But on the assumption of dialectical laws valid for both historical and natural development,[299] it would seem that one could retain the idea of history as nothing but the activity of human agents pursuing their own ends – this activity being the stuff historical motion is made of – *and* subsume it under the general laws of all motion guaranteeing the transition from capitalism to socialism and eventually classless communist society. Thus, it seems that at least at times the logic of this idea about laws of historical development in effect pulled Engels – and Marx[300] – quite close to Althusser's idea about the mode of production

---

[297] Engels, "Engels an Joseph Bloch in Königsberg, 21./22. September 1890", p. 464: "For what each individual wills is obstructed by everyone else, and what emerges is something that no one willed. Thus history has proceeded hitherto in the manner of a natural process and is essentially subject to the same laws of motion.".

[298] Marx & Engels, *Die heilige Familie*, p. 98.

[299] Cf. Engels, *Anti-Dühring*, Appendix, "Notes to Anti-Dühring", p. 436: "In the present work dialectics is conceived as the science of the most general laws of *all* motion. This implies that its laws must be valid just as much for motion in nature and human history as for the motion of thought."

[300] Cf. the Afterword to the 2nd edition of *Capital*, p. 25-27.

producing the different forms of individuality it requires,[301] although with the important difference that while that idea of the self-sustaining mode suggests the eternal reproduction of the mode, and thus renders historical transformations unaccountable for, Marx and Engels assume that the dialectic of forces and relations of production will bring about the transition from capitalism to socialism and eventually classless communist society. What is common to both cases, however, is the effective subordination of agency to quasi-natural *laws* of motion/development, the evacuation of all irreducible efficacy from it.

Not just would this render Engels' and Marx' efforts to further the organisation and revolutionary consciousness of the working class pointless, it should also be obvious that some wills exert a stronger pull than others, and that the *directions* in which wills pull will make a difference too. A Germany turning decisively left rather than right in response to the Great Depression would definitely have made a difference to world history; the policies of the Russian Bolsheviks certainly did.

The only way to escape this dead end would be the postulate, which is indeed found in the quotation from the Russian reviewer in Marx' Afterword to the 2nd edition of *Capital*, and endorsed by Marx, that human wills themselves are determined by quasi-natural laws supposed to rule historical development. But then human agents could not be considered the makers of their own history in any meaningful sense, as they would then be reduced to the mere pawns of those supposed laws. And one would be caught in the same dilemma as that of Althusser and Poulantzas mentioned above: postulating that *all* conceivable societies secrete ideologies "as the very element and atmosphere indispensable to their historical

---

[301] Althusser & Balibar, p. 112.

respiration and life",[302] and that, "Precisely because it is determined by its structure, at the level of experience the social whole remains *opaque* to the agents",[303] one would also have to accept that the social remains opaque to oneself.

So, when trying to account for some historical development, we cannot jump to stating that the actors involved acted in the ways they did either because the laws ruling historical development (or capitalist accumulation or development) made them do it, or, as a variation of that, because it was necessary that they did so if the said development was to take place. We have to explain it in terms of agents' articulation of their experiences and responses, their answers to the question, "who are we, what is our situation, and what can and should be done about it?" and of the struggles between actors over the answers and the choices between them, in the total social context including class (and other) capacities and relations of power, and of course the causes of the opportunities or problems prompting specific responses – that is, the actual interaction between social circumstances and agency in the given context, which is itself to be accounted for in the same way, as itself eventuating from the same interaction.

Social circumstances only develop through this interaction, and agency only through "the *dialogue* between social being and social consciousness",[304] this dialogue being part of the very interaction between social circumstances and agency too. Again, if not for human agency, there would not *be* any historical, but only biological, development, and survival. Human agents' ability to relate consciously and practically to their own existence, to imagine and develop more efficient productive forces and thus change their conditions of life and

---

[302] Althusser, *For Marx*, p. 232.
[303] Poulantzas, p. 207.
[304] Thompson, *The Poverty of Theory and Other Essays*, p. 9.

themselves decisively delimits social history from natural processes. History does *not*, *pace* Engels,[305] make itself.

Marx' and Engels' historical materialism was, and remains, a real and decisive breakthrough, in the first instance in the field of the analysis and critique of capitalism and capitalist society, but also, apart from the very vision of a classless and, in the most real sense, democratic society, in the study of human societies and history generally. That they could not provide sufficient and correct answers to every question in these fields should go without saying, given the inevitable limitation to the historical record up to the final years of the 19th century. It has been, and is, the task of later generations to identify gaps and weaknesses and try to fill the gaps and overcome the weaknesses. But in the attempts to do so, it will not be helpful to pretend that they did not write what they actually wrote.

When dealing with consciousness, we should remember the point made by Thompson: "that consciousness is *lived* as much as it is *known*",[306] and that

> [.....] people do not only experience their own experience as ideas, within thought and its procedures, or (as some theoretical practitioners suppose) as proletarian instinct, etc. They also experience their own experience as *feeling*, and they handle their feelings within their culture, as norms, familial and kinship obligations

---

[305] Engels, "Engels and Joseph Bloch in Königsberg, 21./22. September 1890", p. 464. What Engels argues here about history as a (quasi-) natural process because human wills cancel out is inconsistent with his statement on p. 463 that we make our history ourselves: the laws determining its course are, according to his argument, beyond effective human control. Cf. Thompson, *The Poverty of Theory and Other Essays*, p. 86-87 on this letter from Engels.
[306] Thompson, *The Poverty of Theory and Other Essays*, p. 174.

and reciprocities, as values or (through more elaborated forms) within art or religious beliefs. This half of culture (and it is a full one-half) may be described as affective and moral consciousness.[307]

That is, responses – which are born from consciousness/experience (including the observation of other agents' actions and the assessments and responses they (and those of the agents in question themselves) are met with) – (also) manifest themselves in actual practice (or the lack of it), actual behaviour, in response to a knowledge, or norms, about "what is done" or what is possible or impossible not necessarily explicitly articulated in so many words by agents, but readable from their behaviour or their assessments of the behaviour of others.

The assumption that "we act on what we *think about* the world and our possibilities rather than on the objective facts about them"[308] obviously implies a clear distinction between what we think about the world and our possibilities on the one hand and the *objective facts* about them on the other, these objective facts being irreducible to what we think about them, and what we think about them being irreducible to a mere reflection in our minds about them. It is, therefore in no way to be mistaken for the kind of *de facto* idealism[309] argued by Laclau & Mouffe, who insisted on distinguishing between the *existence* of objects, from which nothing follows,[310] on the one hand and their *being* on the other, and that, "Human beings socially construct their world, and it is through this construction – always precarious and incomplete – that they give to a

---

[307] Thompson, *The Poverty of Theory and Other Essays*, p. 171.

[308] Gram-Jensen, *Structure, Agency and Theory*, p. 15.

[309] A "shame-faced idealism", as Geras called it (Geras, "Post-Marxism?", p. 65; cf. p. 65-67).

[310] Laclau & Mouffe, "Post-Marxism without Apologies", p. 91.

thing its *being*."[311] Laclau & Mouffe rejected the label "ideal-ism".[312] But insofar as they argue that objects do not have any being, are not constituted as objects if not discursively articulated as such, it seems hard to deny that this implies that what reality *is* in any socially and practically relevant sense is constituted by human consciousness, discursively articu-lated.[313] The point is, contrary to this, that we have to *find out* about the relevant objective facts about the world and our possibilities in order to handle them effectively.

As Robinson observed about a specific phenomenon,

> [.....]. Expectations about the future introduce a sub-jective element into the causation of investment which cannot be ruled out, or reduced to simple objective terms, and the fact that human beings learn from ex-perience (though not necessarily aright) means that history itself is an influence upon history."[314]

---

[311] Laclau & Mouffe, *Hegemony and Socialist Strategy*, p. 107-108; "Post-Marxism without Apologies", p. 89. Their assertion that, "[.....] it would be absurd to ask oneself if, outside all scientific the-ory, atomic theory is the 'true being' of matter – the answer will be that atomic theory is a way we have of classifying certain objects, but that these are open to different forms of conceptualization that may emerge in the future. In other words, the 'truth', factual or oth-erwise, about the being of objects is constituted within a theoretical and discursive context, and the idea of a truth outside all context is simply nonsensical" ("Post-Marxism without Apologies", p. 85-86) is obviously self-refuting, inasmuch as the same can be said about their own conceptions of existence, being and truth (cf. Evans, *In Defence of History*, p. 220-221, quoting from Paul Boghossian). Cf. Gram-Jensen, *Structure, Agency and Theory*, Part One, ch. 4, and the fourth essay in *Experience and Historical Materialism*.
[312] Laclau & Mouffe, "Post-Marxism without Apologies", p. 86-89.
[313] Cf. Geras, "Ex-Marxism Without Substance", p. 54-57.
[314] Robinson, p. 94-95.

This is a more narrowly applied formulation of the point that, "we act on what we *think about* the world and our possibilities rather than on the objective facts about them", and that we have to find out about the relevant objective facts about the world and our possibilities, a point which we should never forget. As suggested by the quotation from Robinson, and by this writer,

> The supports of the character masks of capital are under the mute compulsion of capitalism to accumulate capital, but they have to find out *how*, in specific structurally and historically determined conditions and without any guarantee that the line of action they choose is optimal, or even realistic.[315]

In terms of historical explanation, this implies that human agents are not the mere bearers or supports of either illusions or the truth about the world and their possibilities reflected in their brains, but *thinking* agents and actors in a world which is neither transparent nor impenetrably opaque to them, but about aspects of which they may be able to find out, in spite of inevitable errors, gaps and limits; and the decisions and actions of whom we must account for in terms of this interaction between the given social circumstances and agency, with this understanding of the latter.

If we act on what we *think about* the world and our possibilities rather than on the objective facts about them, given that what we think about the world and our possibilities is, while not *altogether* false, not the full and complete truth about them either, then *what* we think about them is important, whether it is right or wrong – although the effects of objective reality, including the limits to the possible set by it, are of course

---

[315] Gram-Jensen, *A Critique of Mau:* Mute Compulsion *and Other Essays*, p. 150.

irreducible. The idea is not an argument for the independence of thought, its lack of determination by objective reality, but implies that *agency*, in its interaction with (objective) social circumstances, is (also) determined by what we *think* about the world – our consciousness constituting an irreducible link between reality and how we handle it. And a link the development of which is itself shaped by the interaction between social circumstances and agency, and the outcomes eventuating from it. Human agents are irreducibly *conscious* beings and actors, articulating (and re-articulating) their experiences of and responses to their "lived" reality as a – indeed *the* – constituent element of historical development.[316]

As for Robinson's specific statement, the history of human society is certainly *also* a history of the accumulated *experiences*, in all their variations, of human agents, and the ways in which they have affected human consciousness and practice, and hence historical development. And that "history itself is an influence upon history" points to the conception of historical development as an *open-ended* process, every moment of which will, in its concrete eventuation from the interaction between social circumstances and agency, impose conditions on subsequent developments, as it delimits the field of the possible, with pressures and probabilities, within which these developments take place.

---

[316] Cf. Thompson, *The Poverty of Theory and Other Essays*, p. 8: "Experience arises spontaneously within social being, but it does not arise without thought; it arises because men and women [.....] are rational, and they think about what is happening to themselves and their world. [.....] For we cannot conceive of any form of social being independently of its organising concepts and expectations, nor could social being reproduce itself for a day without thought."

10. Concluding Remarks.

We cannot rid historical materialism of the idea of laws ruling historical development by excising post-1883 Engels: as documented by Marx' Afterword to the 2nd edition of *Capital* as well as the very conception of the dialectic of forces and relations of production as the motive power of historical development and transformations and the predictions of the inevitable transition from capitalism to socialism and eventually classless communist society, from the mid-1840s and on, Marx too held this idea.

Nor can the idea of quasi-natural laws ruling historical development as offered in Engels' 1890 letter to Bloch be brushed aside as a casual one occasioned by the letter from Bloch to which Engels responds. Already in *Anti-Dühring*, Engels had, as quoted in *A Revised Historical Materialism*, written that,

> The perception of the fundamental contradiction in German idealism led necessarily back to materialism, but, *nota bene*, not to the simply metaphysical, exclusively mechanical materialism of the eighteenth century. In contrast to the naively revolutionary, simple rejection of all previous history, modern materialism sees in the latter the process of evolution of humanity, it being its task to discover the laws of motion thereof.[317]

In *Ludwig Feuerbach und der Ausgang der klassischen deutschen Philosophie*, he wrote that,

---

[317] Engels, *Anti-Dühring*, p. 35 (*MEW*, 20, p. 24); *Die Entwicklung des Sozialismus von der Utopie zur Wissenschaft*, p. 207. Gram-Jensen, *A Revised Historical Materialism*, p. 34.

Now, however, the history of the development of society turns out to be fundamentally [*wesentlich*] different from that of nature. In nature, it is – insofar as we ignore the repercussion of human beings on nature – nothing but unconscious blind agencies affecting each other and in the interaction of which the general law asserts itself. Of all that happens – neither of the countless seemingly accidental occurrences which become visible on the surface, nor of the final results confirming the regularity within these accidental occurrences – nothing happens as a willed conscious end. In the history of society, on the contrary, the actors are nothing but human beings endowed with consciousness, acting with deliberation or passion, aiming at specific ends; nothing happens without a conscious intention, without a willed purpose. But this difference, however important it is for the historical investigation of especially single epochs and events, cannot change anything about the fact that the course of history is ruled by inner general laws. Because in spite of the consciously willed purposes of all individuals, accident rules on the surface even here. What is willed happens only rarely, in most cases the numerous willed ends intersect and struggle with each other, or these ends are impracticable from the outset, or the means inadequate. In this way the clashes between the countless individual wills and individual actions in the historical sphere bring about a state of things wholly analogous to that obtaining in unconscious nature. The ends of the actions are willed, but the results actually resulting from the actions are not willed, or insofar as they nevertheless momentarily seem to correspond to the willed end, they will eventually have consequences quite different from the willed ones. Thus, the historical events likewise seem to be very largely ruled by accident. But everybody playing on the surface of

190

accident will always be controlled by internal hidden laws, and what matters is only to discover these laws.[318]

Finally, in a letter written in January 1894, he wrote that,

1. What we understand by the economic relations, which we regard as the determining basis of the history of society, is the manner and method by which men in a given society produce their means of subsistence and exchange the products among themselves (in so far as division of labour exists). Thus the *entire technique* of production and transport is here included. According to our conception this technique also determines the manner and method of exchange and, further, of the distribution of products and with it, after the dissolution of gentile society, also the division into classes, and hence the relations of lordship and servitude and with them the state, politics, law, etc. Further included in economic relations are the *geographical basis* on which they operate and those remnants of earlier stages of economic development which have actually been transmitted and have survived – often only through tradition or by force of inertia; also of course the external environment which surrounds this form of society.

[.....]

2. We regard economic conditions as that which ultimately conditions historical development. But race is

---

[318] Engels, *Ludwig Feuerbach und der Ausgang der klassischen deutschen Philosophie*, p. 296-297; cf. ch. IV, passim. Quoted in Gram-Jensen, *A Revised Historical Materialism*, p. 35-36.

itself an economic factor. Here, however, two points must not be overlooked:

a) Political, juridical, philosophical, religious, literary, artistic, etc., development is based on economic development. But all these react upon one another and also upon the economic basis. It is not that the economic situation is *cause, solely active*, while everything else is only passive effect. There is, rather, interaction on the basis of economic necessity, which *ultimately* asserts itself. [.....] So it is not, as people try here and there conveniently to imagine, that the economic situation produces an automatic effect. No. Men make their history themselves, only they do so in a given environment, which conditions it, and on the basis of actual relations already existing, among which the economic relations, however much they may be influenced by the other – the political and ideological relations, are still ultimately the decisive ones, forming the keynote which runs through them and alone leads to understanding.

b) Men make their history themselves, but not as yet with a collective will according to a collective plan, or even in a definite, delimited given society. Their aspirations clash, and for that very reason all such societies are governed by *necessity*, the complement and form of appearance of which is *accident*. The necessity which here asserts itself athwart all accident is again ultimately economic necessity. [.....].

So with all the other accidents, and apparent accidents, of history. The further the particular sphere which we are investigating is removed from the economic sphere and approaches that of pure abstract ideology, the more shall we find it exhibiting accidents in its development, the more will its curve run zigzag. But if you plot the average axis of the curve, you will find that this axis will run more and more nearly parallel to the axis of economic development the longer the period considered and the wider the field dealt with.[319]

So, both before and after Engels wrote his letter to Bloch, he argued the notion of history as lawed and that of the relationship between human wills and the laws ruling historical development expressed in this letter. And finally, there is a distinct similarity between this argument and that made on Marx' method by the Russian reviewer quoted and approved by Marx in the Afterword to the 2nd edition of *Capital*: human agents are the makers of their own history, but the actual course of history is nevertheless determined by laws comparable to those ruling natural development rather than by the wills of human agents – either because these wills cancel out, or because they are themselves determined by the said laws.

Not only are no empirical data offered to support Engels' notion about human wills cancelling out, allowing things to develop according to the laws ruling historical development. It is also, in effect, gainsaid by Marx' account of the struggles over the working day according to which workers' resolution and their alliances with political fractions of the British upper classes made possible by political conjunctures *did* make a difference.[320] And in effect gainsaid by Marx' words about the "absolute, general law of capitalist accumulation" quoted above that, *"This is the absolute, general law of capitalist accumulation.* Like all other laws it is modified in its eventuation by

---

[319] Engels, "Engels an W. Borgius in Breslau, 25. Januar 1894", p. 205-207. Quoted in Gram-Jensen, *A Revised Historical Materialism*, p. 29-31.
[320] Marx, *Das Kapital*, 1, ch. 8.6, passim and p. 298, p. p. 300, p. 302, p. 309, p. 311-313.

manifold circumstances the analysis of which does not belong here."[321]

Rather than human wills cancelling out, thus allowing quasi-natural laws to determine historical development, this suggests that the developmental logic of the capitalist mode of production *interacts* with concrete circumstances as well as with agency which thus, along with the concrete circumstances, modifies the effects of the logic, albeit within limits to the possible set by the mode and its developmental logic – and may conceivably, in certain circumstances, make the difference between the very maintenance or abolition of the mode.

In *A Revised Historical Materialism*, there was a quotation from Lakatos:

> *Mature science consists of research programmes in which not only novel facts but, in an important sense, also novel auxiliary theories, are anticipated; mature science – unlike pedestrian trial-and-error – has 'heuristic power'.* Let us remember that in the positive heuristic of a powerful programme there is, right at the start, a general outline of how to build the protective belts: this heuristic power generates *the autonomy of theoretical science.*

> This *requirement of continuous growth* is my rational reconstruction of the widely acknowledged requirement of 'unity' or 'beauty' of science. It highlights the weakness of *two* – apparently very different – types of theorizing. First, it shows up the weakness of programmes which, like Marxism or Freudism, are, no doubt, 'unified',

---

[321] Marx, *Das Kapital*, 1, p. 673-674. This also suggests the distance between the structural analysis of *Capital* and historical analysis. As mentioned, according to Witt-Hansen (p. 115) "absolute" is used by Marx in the Hegelian sense: "abstract".

which give a major sketch of the sort of auxiliary theories they are going to use in absorbing anomalies, but which unfailingly devise their actual auxiliary theories in the wake of facts without, at the same time, anticipating others. (What *novel* fact has Marxism *predicted* since, say, 1917?)[322]

As suggested in the same section of the essay, precise predictions of historical development are, according to the revised historical materialism (considered as a research programme), hard to make; but the conception of historical development as the interaction between social circumstances and agency is predicted to provide the most cogent explanation of the actual historical development. After all, according to this conception human history is not comparable to a natural process (contrary to what e. g. the Afterword to the 2nd edition of *Capital* and passages in Engels suggest).

On this point, then, the revised historical materialism is comparable to the revised Darwinian theory of the origin of species, which cannot predict *what* mutations will occur, *when* they will occur and with *what* effects on the development of species, but is certainly able to *account for* this development. Both are of necessity backward-looking rather than predictive as well as, of course, different from each other in many ways, although the unpredictability of agents' articulation of their experiences of and responses to their "lived" reality and that of mutations may be considered analogous. Rather than the (successful) prediction of novel facts, what we can demand from them is that they are able to tell us what *kind* of process the development of species and historical development respectively is, and to account for the specific outcomes of

---

[322] Lakatos & Musgrave, p. 175-176. Gram-Jensen, *A Revised Historical Materialism*, p. 107.

these processes – not in terms of why they *had to* eventuate according to some law, but in terms of their actual causes.[323]

One implication of the argument made here is that the process of historical development, the interaction between social circumstances and agency, is a continuous, open-ended, unique process of constant change and constantly changing delimitation of a field of the possible, with pressures and probabilities, with social circumstances as well as agents' articulation of their experiences of and responses to their "lived" reality as interacting determinants. It is open-ended because this articulation of experiences and responses cannot be precisely predicted, and may indeed conceivably take unforeseeable turns. And it is unique because the precise actual outcome of the interaction between social circumstances and agency at any precise point in time and space will delimit a specific field of the possible, with subsequent delimitation depending on the precise actual outcome of the interaction between social circumstances and agency within this specific field. Which also means that the precise actual wills contending within that field, and the precise actual relation of strength between them will make a difference in terms of the field of the possible, with its pressures and probabilities, and of the actual outcome – contrary to Engels' idea that the contending

---

[323] Gould argues that, "Fitness – in this context, superior adaptation – cannot be defined after the fact by survival, but must be predictable before the challenge by an analysis of form, physiology, or behavior. As Darwin argued, the deer that should run faster and longer (as indicated by an analysis of bones, joints, and muscles) ought to survive better in a world of dangerous predators. Better survival is a prediction to be tested, not a definition of adaptation." (Gould, *Wonderful Life*, p. 236). But again, this is not a matter of reference to some *law* that the superior variety had to come into existence and survive, but one of a non-circular explanation why this particular variety would, in the given environment, have better chances of survival.

196

wills cancel out, thus allowing quasi-natural laws of social development to determine that outcome "in the manner of a natural process".[324] Which, in its turn, implies, as Thompson put it, "that the project of Socialism is guaranteed *BY NOTHING* – certainly not by "Science" or by Marxism-Leninism – but can find its own guarantees only by *reason* and through an open *choice of values*."[325]

Capitalism is, quite obviously, a major determinant of modern societies, the modern world and its historical development, and analysing capital "so to speak on its ideal average"[326] will enable us to grasp that development much better – but we cannot grasp it *solely* by analysing capital "so to speak on its ideal average" *only*, because other factors will be at work too: *struggles* over interests, including ideological struggles,[327] conflicts or cooperation between states, technological developments, etcetera. The hour of capital on its ideal average never strikes, because social circumstances will interact with *agency*, and the specific conditions of social formations and historical conjunctures will exert an influence on that interaction. Again, the unique, open-ended process of historical development will continuously set and change the limits of the field of the possible and create, change and eliminate pressures and probabilities within these limits of the field of the possible, its actual course developing in this particular, and changing, field. Hence the *specific* experiences and responses agents – *we* – articulate, acting on what we think about the world and our possibilities, will make a real difference to historical development, which eventuates from the interaction

---

[324] Engels, "Engels an Joseph Bloch in Königsberg, 21./22. September 1890", p. 464.

[325] Thompson, *The Poverty of Theory and Other Essays*, p. 171.

[326] Marx, *Das Kapital*, 3, p. 839.

[327] What we think about the world, and act on, is itself the object of, and shaped by, ideological struggles, although objective circumstances will set limits to the possible in this regard.

between social circumstances and agency within the given field of the possible – that is, on the conditions eventuating from the very course of this interaction/development.

The tension between the assumption of *laws* of historical development and transformations independent of and determining the will, consciousness and intentions of human agents[328] on the one hand and that of agents making their own history pursuing their own ends, although on given conditions and with the traditions of the dead generations weighing like a nightmare on their minds, on the other[329] is inherent in Marx' and Engels' historical materialism. Again, one problematical point is that if the will, consciousness and intentions of human agents are determined by the laws of historical development and transformations, as part of a process comparable to that of natural development, this must be true of this historical materialism as well; and if so, the question of its *validity* becomes meaningless, or at least impossible to answer by means of rational argument: whether agents accept or reject it will be determined by the laws of historical development and transformations, just like its formation in the heads of its authors was.[330] If so, it is not even true that society may shorten and alleviate the birthpangs of historical development if it "has got on the scent of the natural law of its motion",[331] because whether or not it gets on this scent *and*

---

[328] Marx, *Das Kapital*, 1, p. 25-26.
[329] Marx & Engels, *Die heilige Familie*, p. 98 (cf. *Die deutsche Ideologie*, p. 45). Marx, *The Eighteenth Brumaire of Louis Bonaparte*, p. 146 (*MEW*, 8, p. 115).
[330] Cf. Favrholdt, p. 159, p. 281-283. Gram-Jensen, *Experience and Historical Materialism*, p. 172-188.
[331] Marx, *Das Kapital*, 1, p. 15-16; cf. p. 12. Marx explicitly states that according to his conception of the development of the economic social formation as a process of natural history, no individual can be held responsible for the conditions the product [*Geschöpf*] of which he remains socially (p. 16). His statement that he welcomes

whether or not agents choose to act on this knowledge and understand how to do so effectively will depend on these same laws.

There is no reason to enter into the consequences of this logical inconsistency in Marx' dialectical method, another crucial element of which is of course the conception of the dialectic of forces and relations of production as the motive power of historical development and transformations – rather than the interaction between social circumstances and agency being conceived as this motive power, which in its turn suggests the importance of agents' articulation of their experiences of and responses to their "lived" reality once the idea that this articulation is determined by quasi-natural laws of development determining the will, consciousness and intentions of agents, that is, these very experiences and responses, is abandoned.

If the process of historical development is considered open-ended, although always within a field of the possible, with pressures and probabilities, delimited by its course up until the given moment, with agents' articulation of their experiences of and responses to their "lived" reality as both eventuating from this process and being a determinant of its further course, the importance of this articulation should be obvious. It is relevant, therefore, to quote the summary of the assumptions about it offered in *Experience and Historical Materialism, Structure, Agency and Theory* and *A Revised Historical Materialism*:

1. What is denoted as the articulation of experiences and responses is, in the final analysis, the articulation of *consciousness* and *social practice*.

---

any scientific critique (p. 17) is, as noted, inconsistent with his assumption that agents' will, consciousness and intentions are determined by quasi-natural laws of historical development.

2. The articulation of experiences is in fact an integral part of agents' responses to "lived" reality, inasmuch as answers to the question: "who are we, what is our situation, what can and should be done about it?" are articulated in and as experience.

3. Experience, then, implies or spells out agents' *horizon of action*: the range of realistic (and (preferably) legitimate) responses they consider open to themselves, whereas their *range of options* denotes the courses of action *objectively* open to them, whether they are aware of it or not.

4. The suggested conception of experiences and responses does not exclude irrationality or subconscious motives. The complex question of defining what can be meant by "irrational" responses and how to distinguish them from "rational" ones (which may be due to misapprehensions of "lived" reality and counterproductive) is not central to the present argument; it must be considered in the context of concrete circumstances and the strategic dimension of agency: a tentative answer could be choosing means which the actor is in a position to know are ill-adapted to objectives, and actions taken from unconscious motives and counterproductive to conscious objectives or to the objectives the actor is in a position to recognise should (or would otherwise) have been chosen in response to the experienced circumstances.

5. As Thompson notes, experience is not only articulated into ideas, in (conscious) thought, but also as *values*, and as "affective and moral consciousness".[332]

---

[332] Thompson, *The Poverty of Theory and Other Essays*, p. 171. Cf. Bourdieu, p. 70: "it is an immediate adherence, at the deepest level of the habitus, to the tastes and distastes, sympathies and aversions, fantasies and phobias which, more than declared opinions, forge the unconscious unity of a class."

Hence struggles over, and adaptations and rearticulations of, responses may be (partly or wholly) in such terms. Moreover "consciousness is *lived* as much as it is *known*."[333]

6. As a means of *handling* social being experience is necessarily interpretative and selective, and hence approximate relative to the "lived" reality it serves to structure for agents. Handling social being also means to make it livable for agents. Just as this may be done more or less effectively by adapting social being to values, values may be (re)interpreted to match perceived reality, or the perception of "lived" reality may be adapted to make it legitimate in the consciousness of agents.

7. On the other hand, the articulation of experiences and responses cannot, for the same reason, simply be *arbitrary* relative to "lived" reality. Experiences and ideological systems and elements are only *relevant* to actors insofar as they can serve to *make sense of* "lived" reality and point to responses (whether objectively rational or not). *The immanent strategic dimension of agency implied by this must be considered an irreducible co-determinant of the articulation of experiences and responses.*

8. Historical development is causally irreducible to the articulation of experiences and responses (including the interaction between different, more or less conflicting, responses): *objective conditions* are determinants (in the last instance) of that articulation, and *interact* with responses to produce the actual outcome of social practice.

---

[333] Thompson, *The Poverty of Theory and Other Essays*, p. 174. Cf. p. 171, p. 175 on the routinisation of responses, and the embodiment of ideology in discursive forms, institutions and rituals.

9. Insofar as historical outcomes are thus irreducible to *intentions*, they may challenge existing values (ideologies).
10. Insofar as agents' positions in the structure of classes (and fractions etcetera) affect their objective conditions, or "lived" reality (what agents do, the probability of various things happening to them (unemployment, bankruptcy, accidents, destitution etcetera etcetera), levels of income, status, power, education..... etcetera), they are also determinants (in the last instance) of their articulation of experiences and responses.
11. Insofar as there are different values or ideologies, different agents are likely to respond in different ways to historical circumstances, processes and outcomes.
12. Insofar as historical outcomes affect agents in different positions in different ways, they may challenge existing values (ideologies).
13. To what extent agents' experiences and responses correspond to their *objective interests* cannot be determined *a priori*. No inherent mechanism in the process of determination guarantees that they do, or that they do not. The specific ensemble of conditions for the articulation of experiences and responses obtaining for specific groups of agents (classes, fractions etcetera) will determine the limits and possibilities in this regard. Which is another way of saying that there is no guarantee that agents will necessarily *act on* their objective interests – or that they *never* will.
14. Part of handling social being is *struggles* over various objectives (conflicting responses); hence the ability to shape the articulation of experiences and responses, and the limits and pressures imposed by objective conditions, are aspects of this context of struggles and *power*.

15. The suggested conception of the interaction between social circumstances and agency implies an element of *unpredictability* in the process of historical development. In the first place, actors are able to learn from experience and hence modify their responses accordingly.[334] Secondly, insofar as the range of possible responses delimited by the ensemble of identifiable determinants is not down to one, several responses may eventuate, with different effects on the actual outcome. And thirdly, *novel* (or more precisely intrinsically new)[335] experiences and responses may be articulated. All of this means that the actual development may be accounted for, but cannot be predicted except with various degrees of uncertainty. *History is open-ended, though not arbitrary.*[336]

Agents may in fact (often) choose between different ways of handling their "lived" reality, in which context it is necessary to distinguish between their objective *range of options* on the one hand and their subjective *horizon of action* on the other. They must be assumed to choose according to their

---

[334] Cf. Carr, *What Is History?*, p. 70-71: "One reason why history rarely repeats itself among historically conscious people is that the dramatis personae are aware at the second performance of the denouement of the first, and their action is affected by that knowledge." By way of illustration, he adds that, "The Bolsheviks knew that the French revolution had ended in a Napoleon, and feared that their own revolution might end in the same way. They therefore mistrusted Trotsky, who among their leaders looked most like a Napoleon, and trusted Stalin, who looked least like a Napoleon."

[335] Cf. Popper, *The Poverty of Historicism*, p. 10, for the distinction between intrinsic newness and novelty of arrangement.

[336] Gram-Jensen, *Experience and Historical Materialism*, p. 141-145; *Structure, Agency and Theory*, p. 280-283; *A Revised Historical Materialism*, p. 74-78.

conception of who they are, what their situation is, and what can and should be done about it – that is, *what* class or other group they belong to, to *whom* they owe solidarity or are opposed, *what*, if anything, it is realistic and legitimate to do about their situation as a group or individually – change it, defend it, or passively accept it.[337]

Human thinking and practice inevitably start within a given material and mental[338] context; but the context may be modified with new ideas and practices, e. g. because of changing conditions or the articulation of new solutions (experiences and responses). These changes will be accountable for in terms of the social circumstances in the context of which they take place, but neither their occurrence, nor their precise nature, are necessarily *predictable* or *derivable* from this context.

Thus, historical development will always take place within the field of the possible, with its pressures and probabilities, delimited by the course of history until the present moment.[339] But the interaction of agents' actual responses to their "lived" reality at that moment with each other and the objective social circumstances will still determine *which* of the potential outcomes within the given field of the possible actually eventuates.

It will rarely, if ever, be only *one* will which dictates the development; but the actual, concrete plurality of wills, *what* they are, and the relative strength of the agents/actors acting on

---

[337] Cf. Gram-Jensen, *A Critique of Mau:* Mute Compulsion *and Other Essays*, p. 140.

[338] Knowledge, beliefs, norms, traditions and collective and individual memories.

[339] Of course, the totality of conditions includes the *natural* conditions of human life, human beings' metabolism with nature and its consequences being a core element of historical development and its conditions, as the climate crisis has made only too obvious.

them will determine the consequences of the struggles between them. On the assumption that agents' will, consciousness and intentions are irreducible to effects of laws of historical development and transitions, actual historical development and transitions must, therefore, be considered irreducible to effects of such (quasi-natural) laws, and historical development and transformations must be considered processes of a unique kind, fundamentally different from law-determined natural ones. And the interaction between social circumstances and human agency should therefore be substituted for the dialectic of forces and relations of production as the assumed motive power of historical development and transformations.

Marx' and Engels' historical materialism offers a general theory on how to grasp and account for the history or prehistory of human society, its development and the transitions from one mode of production and type of society to another, how to explain the capitalist mode of production and exploitation and the promise of the transition from capitalism to socialism and eventually classless communist society constituting the leap from the realm of necessity to the realm of freedom, from the prehistory to the history of human society.[340]

It stands to reason that an untenable conception of the motive power of historical development and transformations is not a suitable basis for dealing with the question of the transition from capitalism to socialism and eventually classless communist society which is the ultimate point of Marx' and Engels' historical materialism and the analysis of *Capital*. It is, therefore, not surprising that the necessity for a revision of this historical materialism is obvious in this context.

---

[340] Marx, *A Contribution to the Critique of Political Economy*, p. 21-22 (*MEW*, 13, p. 9). Engels, *Anti-Dühring*, p. 335-336 (*MEW*, 20, p. 264).

Again, the critique of capitalism as an exploitative, antagonistic, alienating and crisis-ridden mode of production, and the idea of its substitution by socialism and eventually classless communist society defined by the collective command of the means, process and outcome of production as the only real alternative by which the ills of capitalism can be transcended and the potential for human freedom created by the development of the productive forces and the growth in human knowledge be realised, are accepted as correct. The position from which the revision is suggested is thus that of *revolutionary socialism*, not some kind of social-democratic, bourgeois or petty-bourgeois one.

The case against capitalism hardly needs to be made: it is an exploitative, antagonistic, alienating and crisis-ridden mode of production the nature of which is to produce economic inequality,[341] and hence also inequality of status and political influence and power, in spite of its compatibility with bourgeois democracy and thus formal political equality.[342]

As for socialism and communism, there seems to be no alternative to the establishment of the effectively collective command of the means, process and outcome of production as a way of eliminating exploitation and class divisions, but how is it to be organised, and how is it made effective as a mode of *production* and *distribution* to secure the *sustainable* material reproduction and welfare of society at a sufficiently high level? And this as likely as not in a situation with *resistance*, whether armed or "only" by economic and political means, from within and without? The hints in Marx and Engels are few and general, basically making it clear that they envisaged a planned economy with distribution initially according to the

---

341 As argued by Piketty.
342 Therborn.

amount of work delivered and eventually according to the principle, from each according to ability, to each according to needs.[343] Which can hardly be said to go very far in terms of the way in which plans are elaborated and agreed upon, with a sufficiently effective adaptation of production to collective and individual needs, while at the same time the effectively collective nature of decisions is ensured.[344]

It may plausibly be argued that the achievement of a planned economy should not be measured only by the quantity, quality and variety of consumer goods and services it makes available, but also, and primarily, in terms of its sustainability and the level and quality of social security it provides. But it can hardly be argued that the *efficiency* of production and distribution is not important – among other things because it should maximise free time and minimise drudgery and industrial injury, *and* precisely because it should be sustainable and thus minimise pollution and waste, that is, the production of unwanted or unusable products, or the unnecessary expenditure of energy and materials.[345]

At the same time, the length of the period in which *capitalist* production is still the basis of, and hence a condition for, the material reproduction of society, must for obvious reasons be brought to an end as soon as possible, in order to break its stranglehold on state and society, part of which is the structural determination of the state which means that insofar as capitalist production is the dominant form of the material reproduction of society, the state is reduced to a role and functioning that is compatible with the fundamental interest of the capitalist class: the maintenance of capitalist relations of

---

343 Marx, "Kritik des Gothaer Programms", p. 21.
344 Cf. Miliband, p. 66.
345 Cf. Nove, p. 82, p. 101.

production and capitalist exploitation.[346] *Both* production and the process of decision-making on production, and public affairs generally, have to be revolutionised, which will in itself be likely to produce serious complications and involve trial, error and corrections. It may formally be done at a stroke by decree, but to make both *work* effectively is another thing. And the risk of a de facto centralisation of the command of the means, process and outcome of production must be effectively countered to avoid a repetition of post-1917 "real existing socialism". It was hardly unfair when Miliband observed that, "Marxists and socialists in general have always tended to underestimate the problems that must arise in the organization of a post-capitalist society."[347] This is not to suggest that these problems are insoluble, but they should be recognised, answers should be found and countermeasures taken by revolutionary-socialist organisations *before* the transition from capitalism to socialism is made – with the full consciousness that adaptations will no doubt have to be made afterwards.

One point can be considered certain: neither a *reformist* nor a *gradualist* strategy as defined in *Structure, Agency and Theory* is a solution: the former is limited to reforms meant to improve working-class conditions without challenging the capitalist framework,[348] which does not abolish capitalist exploitation or break the dependence of the material reproduction of society on capitalist production, and working-class gains may always be rolled back and are vulnerable to crises and capitalist disinvestment once reforms are hurting profits. The latter is a strategy of continuous extension of reforms cumulatively leading to the gradual transcending of capitalism and so into

---

[346] Gram-Jensen, *Structure, Agency and Theory*, Part Three, ch. 7. c; p. 1334-1335.
[347] Miliband, p. 67.
[348] Gram-Jensen, *Structure, Agency and Theory*, p. 1333.

socialism,[349] which prolongs the period of dependence on capitalist production, and thus suffers from the same weaknesses as the former.[350] No strategy for the transition from capitalism to socialism and eventually classless communist society can evade the absolute necessity of breaking the dependence of state and society on capitalist production and thus the power of the capitalist class. As observed in *Structure, Agency and Theory*,

> [U]ntil an alternative, socialist framework has been established, state and economy have to function according to the capitalist one, and thus exploitation and the demands on economic efficiency in the capitalist sense have to be continued if the material reproduction of society is not to be jeopardised. Assuming that this gradualist strategy has as its central plank a gradual process of de-privatisation of business, the means of resistance to any reforms even remotely dangerous to the capitalist social order thus left in the hand of capitalist and bourgeois actors will be formidable: as long as the private (capitalist) sector remains decisive in terms of the material reproduction of society (at a certain level), its owners will be in a position to threaten, or if necessary stop, that reproduction and hence stalemate gradualist policies. Even apart from such purposeful resistance, it is hard to see how a high level of performance of a capitalist economy can be combined with the gradual supersession of the capitalist structure of that same economy over a lengthy period of time, as there would be no rational incentive for owners of capital to invest in it.

---

[349] Gram-Jensen, *Structure, Agency and Theory*, p. 1330.
[350] Gram-Jensen, *Structure, Agency and Theory*, Part Three, ch. 7. c.

Thus, as production grinds to a halt, unemployment spreads and standards of living plummet, a gradualist movement would have only the choice between embarking on the (revolutionary) transition to an alternative framework of material reproduction, or giving up its gradualist aspirations to become a mere movement for reforms within the capitalist social order. Ideologically and practically ill-prepared for the former, it would be likely to choose the latter. If it did in fact choose the former, it would have to accomplish the task effectively and quickly enough to prevent a crisis too deep and protracted for the movement to retain the support of a majority; failing to do so, it would have to give up political power and its project of transition, or it would have to try to accomplish it without majority support, and hence by undemocratic means, thus blocking the way to a really *socialist* society and hence to the collective command of the means, process and outcome of production. It goes without saying that a revolutionary-socialist movement failing to maintain a sufficiently high level of material reproduction on a *socialist* basis would face the same dilemma: whether it chose to accept the capitalist social order or to transcend it, a transition to *socialism*, and eventually communism, would be blocked.[351]

One might say that the "mute compulsion" of the economic conditions,[352] which Mau has very meritoriously emphasised,[353] seals the domination of the capitalists not just over the working class, but over the state and the whole of society as well.[354]

---

[351] Gram-Jensen, *Structure, Agency and Theory*, p. 872-873.
[352] Marx, *Das Kapital*, 1, p. 765.
[353] Mau, p. 3 ff and passim.
[354] Cf. Parsons, p. 491-492.

Marx' and Engels' historical materialism gives the promise that the said transition *can* and *will* be accomplished, according to the laws of historical development and transformations. And history has amply demonstrated the questionable nature of their expectations and predictions. As for Engels' parallelograms of forces, the interactions of individual (and collective) wills have not made them cancel out and thus let laws of historical development take the development of advanced capitalist societies in the predicted direction.

The isolation of class struggle, the divisions splitting the working class, the political developments in advanced capitalist societies, the conflicts between them, the different varieties of "welfare states", the complexities of the development of these societies in general, and the trajectory of "real existing socialism" is more cogently explained on the basis of the conception of the interaction between social circumstances and agency as the motive power of historical development and transformations than on the basis of the conception of the dialectic of forces and relations of production as that motive power.

In other words, the question of the right strategy for the transition is irreducible to the return to the genuine vision of Marx and Engels, the rediscovery of their strategy for the revolution, because in effect no such strategy can be found in their texts – which do indeed contain pointers, but no coherent and realistic strategy – quite logically on the basis of the assumption that the mere vision of classless society demonstrates its feasibility,[355] and that historical development is ruled by laws determining the will, consciousness and intentions of agents. And it is imperative that the problems left

[355] Marx, *A Contribution to the Critique of Political Economy*, p. 21 (*MEW*, 13, p. 9).

unsolved or unrecognised are discussed without prejudice or inhibitions.

Today, it seems only too obvious that the "realm of freedom" which Engels sketched in such glowing terms in *Anti-Dühring*[356] will inevitably, and quite apart from the necessary work which cannot be taken over by machines or robots, be limited by necessity, at least in any foreseeable future: not in the sense that effective democracy is impossible to establish, but by the necessity of sustainability: it will simply not be possible for an unlimited number of human beings to live in material wealth without considering the limited resources of the earth and the effects on the climate. Future advances in knowledge and technology may minimise the realm of necessity, but it cannot be completely eliminated: human existence will always imply *conditions* for the satisfaction of needs and desires and the survival of the species. And even with the effectively collective control of the means, process and outcome of production firmly established in classless communist society, this has to be recognised and handled.

At least three large, and interrelated, questions about the transition from capitalism to socialism and eventually classless communist society have not, so far, been convincingly answered:

1. How to mobilise and organise a majority of (the working class and) the population for this transition, and how to accomplish that transition in a way actually making the establishment of the effectively collective command of the means, process and outcome of production possible.
2. How to organise public decision-making in a way which makes decision-making and administration

---

[356] Engels, *Anti-Dühring*, p. 335-336 (*MEW*, 20, p. 264).

both efficient and a means of the effectively collective command of the means, process and outcome of production.

3. How to organise production and distribution consistently with the effectively collective command of the means, process and outcome of production and with the principle "from each according to ability and to each according to need", *and* the demand for sustainability.

As a fourth major question one may mention the handling of *international* relations and conflicts, focusing on justice, equality and development and, not least, the avoidance of war and the establishment of effective organs for the peaceful settlement of conflicts between social formations.

All the above arguments do not mean that the transition from capitalism to socialism and eventually classless communist society is necessarily *impossible*; but rather that it is not *guaranteed* by any laws of historical development and transformations; that it involves great difficulties and dangerous pitfalls; and that it will make a real difference *how* we set about it.

Appendix: From the *Grundrisse*.

In Appendix Three in *Structure, Agency and Theory*, only the 17th of the passages quoted below was included as evidence of Marx' and Engels' determinism in the sense of their expectations and predictions that the dialectic of forces and relations of production, which they conceived as the motive power of historical development and transformations, made the transition from capitalism to socialism and eventually classless communist society inevitable. To supplement that evidence, 16 more passages are quoted here from the *Grundrisse*.

1. p. 159:
[.....]. But within bourgeois society, the society that rests on *exchange value*, there arise relations of circulation as well as of production which are so many mines to explode it. (A mass of antithetical forms of the social unity, whose anti-thetical character can never be abolished through quiet metamorphosis. On the other hand, if we did not find concealed in society as it is the material conditions of production and the corresponding relations of exchange prerequisite for a classless society, then all attempts to explode it would be quixotic.)

2. p. 278:
[.....]. It must be kept in mind that the new forces of production and relations of production do not develop out of *nothing*, nor drop from the sky, nor from the womb of the self-positing Idea; but from within and in antithesis to the existing development of production and the inherited, traditional relations of property.

3. p. 325:

The great historic quality of capital is to create this *surplus labour*, superfluous labour from the standpoint of mere use value, mere subsistence; and its historic destiny [*Bestimmung*] is fulfilled as soon as, on one side, there has been such a development of needs that surplus labour above and beyond necessity has itself become a general need arising out of individual needs themselves – and, on the other side, when the severe discipline of capital, acting on succeeding generations [*Geschlechter*], has developed general industriousness as the general property of the new species [*Geschlecht*] – and, finally, when the development of the productive powers of labour, which capital incessantly whips onward with its unlimited mania for wealth, and of the sole conditions in which this mania can be realized, have flourished to the stage where the possession and preservation of general wealth require a lesser labour time of society as a whole, and where the labouring society relates scientifically to the process of its progressive reproduction, its reproduction in a constantly greater abundance; hence where labour in which a human being does what a thing could do has ceased. Accordingly, capital and labour relate each other here like money and commodity; the former is the general form of wealth, the other only the substance destined for immediate consumption. Capital's ceaseless striving towards the general form of wealth drives labour beyond the limits of its natural paltriness [*Naturbedürftigkeit*], and thus creates the material elements for the development of the rich individuality which is as all-sided in its production as in its consumption, and whose labour also therefore appears no longer as labour, but as the full development of activity itself, in which natural necessity in its direct form has disappeared; because a historically created need has

216

taken the place of the natural one. This is why *capital is productive; i.e. an essential relation for the development of the social productive forces*. It ceases to exist as such only where the development of these productive forces themselves encounters its barrier in capital itself.

4. p. 410:
But from the fact that capital posits every such limit as a barrier and hence gets *ideally* beyond it, it does not by any means follow that it has *really* overcome it, and, since every such barrier contradicts its character, its production moves in contradictions which are constantly overcome but just as constantly posited. Furthermore. The universality towards which it irresistibly strives encounters barriers in its own nature, which will, at a certain stage of its development, allow it to be recognized as being itself the greatest barrier to this tendency, and hence will drive towards its own suspension.

5. p. 411:
[.....]; while Sismondi, by contrast, emphasises not only the encounter with the barriers, but their creation by capital itself, and has a vague intuition that they must lead to its breakdown."

6. p. 411:
[.....]. On the other side, Ricardo and his entire school never understood the really *modern crises*, in which this contradiction of capital discharges itself in great thunderstorms which increasingly threaten it as the foundation of society and of production itself.

7. p. 415:

[......]. The stages of production which precede capital appear, regarded from its standpoint, as so many fetters upon the productive forces. It itself, however, correctly understood, appears as the condition of the development of the forces of production as long as they require an external spur, which appears at the same time as their bridle. It is a discipline over them, which becomes superfluous and burdensome at a certain level of their development, just like the guilds etc.

8. p. 461:

[......]. Just as, on one side the pre-bourgeois phases appear as *merely historical*, i.e. suspended presuppositions, so do the contemporary conditions of production likewise appear as engaged in *suspending themselves* and hence in positing the *historic presuppositions* for a new state of society.

9. p. 462-463:

[......]. Thus labour capacity's own labour is as alien to it – and it really is, as regards its direction etc. – as are material and instrument. Which is why the product then appears to it as a combination of alien material, alien instrument and alien labour – as *alien property*, and why, after production, it has become poorer by the life forces expended, but otherwise begins the drudgery anew, existing as a mere subjective labour capacity separated from the conditions of its life. The recognition [*Erkennung*] of the products as its own, and the judgment that its separation from the conditions of its realization is improper – forcibly imposed – is an enormous [advance in] awareness [*Bewusstsein*], itself the product of the mode of production resting on capital, and as much the knell to its doom as, with the slave's awareness that he *cannot be the property of another*, with his consciousness of himself as a person, the existence of slavery becomes a merely artificial, vegetative existence, and ceases to be able to prevail as the basis of production.

10. p. 495:
In the last analysis, their community, as well as the property based on it, resolves itself into a specific stage in the development of the productive forces of working subjects – to which correspond their specific relations amongst one another and towards nature. Until a certain point, reproduction. Then turns into dissolution.

11. p. 496-497:
All forms (more or less naturally arisen, spontaneous, all at the same time however results of a historic process) in which the community presupposes its subjects in a specific objective unity with their conditions of production, or in which a specific subjective mode of being presupposes the communities themselves as conditions of production, necessarily correspond to a development of the forces of production which is only limited, and indeed limited in principle. The development of the forces of production dissolves these forms, and their dissolution is itself a development of the human productive forces. Labour begins with a certain foundation – naturally arisen, spontaneous, at first – then historic presupposition. Then, however, this foundation or presupposition is itself suspended, or posited as a vanishing presupposition which has become too confining for the unfolding of the progressing human pack.

12. p. 540:

[.....]. This tendency – which capital possesses, but which at the same time, since capital is a limited form of production, contradicts it and hence drives it towards dissolution – distinguishes capital from all earlier modes of production, and at the same time contains this element, that capital is posited as a mere point of transition.

13. p. 541-542:

[.....]. The barrier to *capital* is that this entire development proceeds in a contradictory way, and that the working-out of the productive forces, of general wealth etc., knowledge etc., appears in such a way that the working individual *alienates* himself [*sich entäussert*]; relates to the conditions brought out of him by his labour as those not of his *own* but of an *alien wealth* and of his own poverty. But this antithetical form is itself fleeting, and produces the real conditions of its own suspension.

14. p. 543:

[.....]. At a certain point, a development of the forces of material production – which is at the same time a development of the forces of the working class – *suspends capital itself.*

15. p. 651:

[.....]. As soon as it [capital – I. G.-J.] feels strong, it throws away the crutches, and moves in accordance with its own laws. As soon as it begins to sense itself and become conscious of itself as a barrier to development, it seeks refuge in forms which, by restricting free competition, seem to make the rule of capital more perfect, but are at the same time the heralds of its dissolution and of the dissolution of the mode of production resting on it.[357]

16. p. 704-706:
The exchange of living labour for objectified labour – i.e. the positing of social labour in the form of the contradiction of capital and wage labour – is the ultimate development of the *value-relation* and of production resting on value. Its presupposition is – and remains – the mass of direct labour time, the quantity of labour employed, as the determinant factor in the production of wealth. But to the degree that large industry develops, the creation of real wealth comes to depend less on labour time and on the amount of labour employed than on the power of the agencies set in motion during labour time, whose 'powerful effectiveness' is itself in turn out of all proportion to the direct labour time spent on their production, but depends rather on the general state of science and on the progress of technology, or the application of this science to production. (The development of this science, especially natural science, and all others with the latter, is itself in turn related to the development of material production.) Agriculture, e.g., becomes merely the application of the science of material metabolism, its regulation for the greatest advantage of the entire body of society. Real wealth manifests itself, rather – and large industry reveals this – in the monstrous disproportion between the labour time applied, and its product, as well as in the qualitative imbalance between labour, reduced to a pure abstraction, and the power of the production

[357] Cf. p. 652: "By the way, when the illusion about competition as the so-called absolute form of free individuality vanishes, this is evidence that the conditions of competition, i.e. of production founded on capital, are already felt and thought of as *barriers*, and hence already *are* such, and more and more become such.

process it superintends. Labour no longer appears so much to be included within the production process; rather, the human being comes to relate more as watchman and regulator to the production process itself. (What holds for machinery holds likewise for the combination of human activities and the development of human intercourse.) No longer does the worker insert a modified natural thing [*Naturgegenstand*] as middle link between the object [*Objekt*] and himself; rather, he inserts the process of nature, transformed into an industrial process, as a means between himself and inorganic nature, mastering it. He steps to the side of the production process instead of being its chief actor. In this transformation, it is neither the direct human labour he himself performs, nor the time during which he works, but rather the appropriation of his own general productive power, his understanding of nature and his mastery over it by virtue of his presence as a social body – it is, in a word, the development of the social individual which appears as the great foundation-stone of production and of wealth. The *theft of alien labour time, on which the present wealth is based,* appears a miserable foundation in face of this new one, created by large-scale industry itself. As soon as labour in the direct form has ceased to be the great well-spring of wealth, labour time ceases and must cease to be its measure, and hence exchange value [must cease to be the measure] of use value. The *surplus labour of the mass* has ceased to be the condition for the development of general wealth, just as the *non-labour of the few*, for the development of the general powers of the human head. With that, production based on exchange value breaks down, and the direct, material production process is stripped of the form of penury and antithesis. The free development of individualities, and hence not the reduction of necessary labour time so as to posit surplus

222

labour, but rather the general reduction of the necessary labour of society to a minimum, which then corresponds to the artistic, scientific etc. development of the individuals in the time set free, and with the means created, for all of them. Capital itself is the moving contradiction, [in] that it presses to reduce labour time to a minimum, while it posits labour time, on the other side, as sole measure and source of wealth. Hence it diminishes labour time in the necessary form so as to increase it in the superfluous form; hence posits the superfluous in growing measure as a condition – question of life and death – for the necessary. On the one side, then, it calls to life all the powers of science and of nature, as of social combination and of social intercourse, in order to make the creation of wealth independent (relatively) of the labour time employed on it. On the other side, it wants to use labour time as the measuring rod for the giant social forces thereby created, and to confine them within the limits required to maintain the already created value as value. Forces of production and social relations – two different sides of the development of the social individual – appear to capital as mere means, and are merely means for it to produce on its limited foundation. In fact, however, they are the material conditions to blow this foundation sky-high. 'Truly wealthy a nation, when the working day is 6 rather than 12 hours. *Wealth* is not command over surplus labour time' (real wealth), 'but rather, *disposable time* outside that needed in direct production, for *every individual* and the whole society.' (*The Source and Remedy*, etc. 1821, p. 6).[358]

---

[358] *The Source and Remedy of the National Difficulties, Deduced from Principles of Political Economy. In a Letter to Lord John Russel.* Anonymous, London 1821.

17. p. 749-750:

[.....]. Beyond a certain point, the development of the powers of production becomes a barrier for capital; hence the capital relation a barrier for the development of the productive powers of labour. When it has reached this point, capital, i.e. wage labour, enters into the same relation towards the development of social wealth and of the forces of production as the guild system, serfdom, slavery, and is necessarily stripped off as a fetter. The last form of servitude assumed by human activity, that of wage labour on one side, capital on the other, is thereby cast off like a skin, and this casting-off itself is the result of the mode of production corresponding to capital; the material and mental conditions of the negation of wage labour and of capital, themselves already the negation of earlier forms of unfree social production, are themselves results of its production process. The growing incompatibility between the productive development of society and its hitherto existing relations of production expresses itself in bitter contradictions, crises, spasms. The violent destruction of capital not by relations external to it, but rather as a condition of its self-preservation, is the most striking form in which advice is given it to be gone and to give room to a higher state of social production.

The context of this passage is Marx' argument on the law of *"the inherent tendency towards the fall of the rate of profit"*[359] which he describes as "in every respect the most important law of modern political economy" and "the most important law from the historical standpoint".[360] It is not necessary to

---

[359] Marx, *Grundrisse*, p. 754; cf. p. 763.
[360] Marx, *Grundrisse*, p. 748.

discuss it in any detail here, but it may be rendered in Marx' own words that,

> Presupposing the same surplus value, *the same surplus labour in proportion to necessary labour*, then, the *rate of profit* depends on the relation between the part of capital exchanged for living labour and the part existing in the form of raw material and means of production. Hence, the smaller the portion exchanged for living labour becomes, the smaller becomes the rate of profit. Thus, in the same proportion as capital takes up a larger place as capital in the production process relative to immediate labour, i.e. the more the relative surplus value grows – the value-creating power of capital – the more *does the rate of profit fall*. We have seen that the magnitude of the capital already presupposed, presupposed to reproduction, is specifically expressed in the growth of fixed capital, as the produced productive force, objectified labour endowed with apparent life. The total value of the producing capital will express itself in each of its portions as a diminished proportion of the capital exchanged for living labour relative to the part of capital existing as constant value.[361]

The law, then, implies that if the value of the fixed, or constant, capital, which does not create value,[362] grows relative to the value of the variable capital (labour), which does create value which is in part appropriated by the owner(s) of capital as surplus value (profit), the rate of profit, i. e. the profit as a

---

[361] Marx, *Grundrisse*, p. 747; cf. p. 763.
[362] "Its use value is precisely that it increases the productive power of labour, decreases necessary labour, and increases relative surplus labour and hence surplus value. To the extent that it enters into circulation, its value is merely replaced, not increased." (Marx, *Grundrisse*, p. 766).

fraction or percentage of the invested capital,[363] will fall, this leading to profitability-crises:

> [.....]. What capital adds is that it increases the surplus labour time of the mass by all the means of art and science, because its wealth consists directly in the appropriation of surplus labour time; since *value directly its purpose*, not use value. It is thus, despite itself, instrumental in creating the means of social disposable time, in order to reduce labour time for the whole society to a diminishing minimum, and thus to free everyone's time for their own development. But its tendency always, on the one side, *to create disposable time, on the other, to convert it into surplus labour*. If it succeeds too well at the first, then it suffers from surplus production, and then necessary labour is interrupted, because *no surplus labour can be realized by capital*. The more this contradiction develops, the more does it become evident that the growth of the forces of production can no longer be bound up with the appropriation of alien labour, but that the mass of workers must themselves appropriate their own surplus labour. Once they have done so – and *disposable time* thereby ceases to have an *antithetical* existence – then, on the one side, necessary labour time will be measured by the needs of the social individual, and, on the other, the development of the power of social production will grow so rapidly that, even though production is now calculated for the wealth of all, *disposable time* will grow for all. For real wealth is the developed productive power of all

---

[363] "*In its immediate form, profit is nothing but the sum of the surplus value expressed as a proportion of the total value of capital.*" (Marx, *Grundrisse*, p. 767).

individuals. The measure of wealth is then not any longer, in any way, labour time, but rather disposable time.[364]

---

[364] Marx, *Grundrisse*, p. 708. "Necessary labour" is that part of the labour going into production the value of which is necessary to maintain the existence and labour-power of the workers, surplus labour is that which is delivered in addition to the necessary labour, and the value of which is appropriated by (the owner(s) of) capital. The passage certainly reflects Marx' confidence in the eventual transition from capitalism to socialism and eventually classless communist society.

References.

Althusser, Louis: *For Marx*. London 1968 [Francois Maspero 1965].

Althusser, Louis & Balibar, Etienne: *Reading Capital*. London 1979 [New Left Books 1970. 2nd Edition Paris 1968].

Anderson, Perry: *Considerations on Western Marxism*. London 1979 [1976].

Anderson, Perry: *Lineages of the Absolutist State*. London 1979 [1974].

Balibar, Etienne: "Self Criticism: An Answer to Questions from 'Theoretical Practice'" Theoretical Practice, no 7-8, January 1973.

Bohr, Niels: *Atomic Physics and Human Knowledge*. Mineola, New York 2010 [København 1957].

Bourdieu, Pierre: *Distinction: A Social Critique of the Judgement of Taste*. London 2010 [1984. Paris 1979].

Carr, E. H.: *What Is History?* Harmondsworth, Middlesex, 1964 [London 1961].

Cohen, Gerald Allan: *Karl Marx's Theory of History: a Defence*. Princeton, New Jersey 1978.

Collier, Andrew: *Marx*. Oxford 2004.

Cutler, Anthony & Hindess, Barry & Hirst, Paul & Hussain, Athar: *Marx's 'Capital' and Capitalism Today*. London 1977-1978.

Darwin, Charles: *The Origin of Species*. New York 1928 [6th Edition 1882 (1st Edition 1859].

Draper, Hal: *Karl Marx's Theory of Revolution*. New York-London 1977-2005.

Draper, Hal: *The Adventures of the Communist Manifesto*. Chicago 2020 [1994].

Engels, Friedrich: *Anti-Dühring. Herr Eugen Dühring's Revolution in Science*. London 1975. *MEW*, 20.

Engels, Friedrich: *Die Entwicklung des Sozialismus von der Utopie zur Wissenschaft*. Berlin 1891[Paris 1880]. *MEW*, 19.

Engels, Friedrich: "Engels an Conrad Schmidt, 5. August 1890" *MEW*, 37.

Engels, Friedrich: "Engels an Conrad Schmidt, 27. Oktober 1890" *MEW*, 37.

Engels, Friedrich: "Engels an Conrad Schmidt, 12. März 1895" *MEW*, 39.

Engels, Friedrich: "Engels an Joseph Bloch in Königsberg, 21./22. September 1890" *MEW*, 37.

Engels, Friedrich: "Engels an Marx in London, 11. oder 12. Dezember 1859" *MEW*, 29.

Engels, Friedrich: "Engels an W. Borgius in Breslau, 25. Januar 1894" *MEW*, 39.

Engels, Friedrich: *Ludwig Feuerbach und der Ausgang der klassischen deutschen Philosophie*. Stuttgart 1888 [*Die Neue Zeit*, Vierter Jahrgang, Nr. 4 und 5, 1886]. *MEW*, 21.

Esping-Andersen, Gösta: *The Three Worlds of Welfare Capitalism*. Cambridge-Oxford 1999.

Evans, Richard J.: *In Defence of History*. London 2000 [1997].

Favrholdt, David: *Filosoffen Niels Bohr*. København 2009.

French, A. P. & Kennedy, P. J. (eds.): *Niels Bohr. A Centenary Volume*. Cambridge, Massachusetts – London 1985.

Gasper, Phil: "Is Marxism Deterministic?" International Socialist Review, Issue 58, March-April 2008, online edition, www.isreview.org/issues/58/gasper-determinism.shtml.

Geras, Norman: *Literature of Revolution: Essays on Marxism*. London 1986.

Geras, Norman: "Post-Marxism?" *New Left Review* no 163, 1987.

Goodin, Robert E. & Headey, Bruce & Muffels, Ruud & Dirven, Hen-Jan: *The Real Worlds of Welfare Capitalism*. Cambridge 1999.

Gould, Stephen Jay: *Wonderful Life: The Burgess Shale and the Nature of History*. London 2000 [1990].

Gram-Jensen, Ib: *A Critique of Mau:* Mute Compulsion *and Other Essays: Seven More Argumentative Essays.* Hellerup 2023.

Gram-Jensen, Ib: *A Revised Historical Materialism: Three More Argumentative Essays.* Hellerup 2024.

Gram-Jensen, Ib: *Experience and Historical Materialism: Five Argumentative Essays.* København 2020.

Gram-Jensen, Ib: *Structure, Agency and Theory: Contributions to Historical Materialism and the Analysis of Classes, State and Bourgeois Power in Advanced Capitalist Societies.* Hellerup 2021.

Gray, Robert: "History, Marxism and Theory" in: Kay, Harvey J. & McClelland, Keith (eds.): *E. P. Thompson: Critical Perspectives.* Cambridge 1990.

Hexter, J. H.: *Doing History.* Bloomington-London 1971.

Hindess, Barry & Hirst, Paul: *Pre-Capitalist Modes of Production.* London 1975.

Hirst, Paul: "Economic Classes and Politics" in: Hunt, Alan (ed.): *Classes and Class Structure.* London 1977.

Hobsbawm, Eric J.: *On History.* London 1998 [1997].

Hobsbawm, Eric J.: *The Age of Empire.* London 1994 [1987].

Jenkins, Keith: *At the Limits of History: Essays on Theory and Practice.* London – New York 2009.

Jenkins, Keith: *Re-thinking History.* London 2003 [1991].

Kaufmann, Walter: "The Hegel Myth and Its Method" [in: Kaufmann, Walter: *From Shakespeare to Existentialism.* Boston 1959 [Published as *The Owl and the Nightingale.* London 1960]].

Koch, Carl Henrik: *Isaac Newton: Geniet og Mennesket.* København 2013.

Laclau, Ernesto & Mouffe, Chantal: *Hegemony and Socialist Strategy. Towards a Radical Democratic Politics.* London 1985.

Laclau, Ernesto & Mouffe, Chantal: "Post-Marxism without Apologies" *New Left Review* no 166, 1987.

Lakatos, Imre & Musgrave, Alan (eds.): *Criticism and the Growth of Knowledge. Proceedings of the International Colloquium in the Philosophy of Science, London 1965, volume 4.* London 1970.

Levine, Andrew & Wright, Erik Olin: "Rationality and Class Struggle" *New Left Review* no 123, 1980.

Marx, Karl: *A Contribution to the Critique of Political Economy.* New York 1970. *MEW*, 13.

Marx, Karl: [Brief an die Redaktion der "Otetschestwennyje Sapiski""] Mew, 19 [1877?].

Marx, Karl: *Das Elend der Philosophie. Antwort auf Proudhons "Philosophie des Elends".* MEW, 4. [Paris-Bruxelles 1847].

Marx, Karl: *Das Kapital. Kritik der politischen Ökonomie. MEW*, 23-24-25 [1867, 1885, 1894].

Marx, Karl: *Der Bürgerkrieg in Frankreich. Adresse des Generalrats der Internationalen Arbeiter-Assoziation.* Berlin 1891 [London 1871]. *MEW*, 17.

Marx, Karl: "Der Generalrat an den Föderalrat der romanischen Schweiz" *MEW*, 16.

Marx, Karl: *Early Writings.* Harmondsworth, Middlesex 1975.

Marx, Karl: *Enthüllungen über den Kommunisten-Prozeß zu Köln.* MEW, 8 [1885 edition. 1st edition Basel-Boston 1853].

Marx, Karl: ["Entwürfe einer Antwort auf den Brief von V. I. Sassulitsch"] *MEW*, 19.

Marx, Karl: *Grundrisse: Foundations of the Critique of Political Economy (Rough Draft).* London 1993 [1973; 1st edition Moscow 1939, 1941].

Marx, Karl: "Inauguraladresse der Internationalen Arbeiter-Assoziation" Der *Sozial-Demokrat* Nr. 2 und 3 vom 21. und 30. Dezember 1864. *MEW*, 16.

Marx, Karl: "Kritik des Gothaer Programms" *MEW*, 19 [1875. *Die Neue Zeit* Nr. 18, 9. Jahrgang, 1890-1891].

Marx, Karl: *Lohn, Preis und Profit. MEW*, 16 [1865].

Marx, Karl: "Marx an Ferdinand Lasalle in Berlin, 16. Januar 1861" *MEW*, 30.

Marx, Karl: "Marx an Pawel Wassiljewitsch Annenkow in Paris, 28. Dezember [1846]" *MEW*, 4.

Marx, Karl: "Marx an Sigfrid Meyer und August Vogt in New York, 9. April 1870" *MEW*, 32.

Marx, Karl, "Provisorische Statuten der Internationalen Arbeiter-Assoziation" *MEW*, 16 [in: *Address and Provisional rules of the Working-Men's International Association…* London 1864. *The Bee-Hive* no 161, 12. 11. 1864].

Marx, Karl: "Rede auf der Jahresfeier des "People's Paper" am 14. April 1856 in London" *MEW*, 12.

Marx, Karl: *The Class Struggles in France: 1848 to 1850*. In: *Surveys from Exile* (edited by David Fernbach) New York 1974. *MEW*, 7.

Marx, Karl: *The Eighteenth Brumaire of Louis Bonaparte*. In: *Surveys from Exile* (edited by David Fernbach) New York 1974. *MEW*, 8.

Marx, Karl: *Zweite Adresse des Generalrats über den Deutsch-Französischen Krieg. MEW*, 17.

Marx, Karl & Engels, Friedrich: *Die deutsche Ideologie. Kritik der neuesten deutschen Philosophie und ihre Repräsentanten, Feuerbach, B. Bauer und Stirner, und des deutschen Sozialismus in seinen verschiedenen Propheten. MEW*, 3.

Marx, Karl & Engels, Friedrich: *Die heilige Familie oder Kritik der kritischen Kritik. Gegen Bruno Bauer und Konsorten. MEW*, 2 [Frankfurt am Main 1845].

Marx, Karl & Engels, Friedrich: *Manifest der Kommunistischen Partei. MEW*, 4. [London 1848].

Marx, Karl & Engels, Friedrich: *Selected Correspondence*. Moscow 1965 (1st edition 1955).

Marx, Karl & Engels, Friedrich: ["Zirkularbrief an Bebel, Liebknecht, Bracke u.a."] *MEW*, 19 [17./18. 9. 1879].

Mau, Søren: *Mute Compulsion: A Marxist Theory of the Economic Power of Capital*. London – New York 1923.

McIntyre, Lee: *Post-Truth*. Cambridge, Massachusetts 2018.

Meiksins Wood, Ellen: *Democracy Against Capitalism: Renewing Historical Materialism*. London 2016 [Cambridge 1995].

Meiksins Wood, Ellen: *The Retreat from Class. A New 'True' Socialism.* London 1986.

Miliband, Ralph: *Socialism for a Sceptical Age.* Cambridge – Oxford 1994.

Mills, C. Wright: *The Marxists.* New York 1962.

Nove, Alec: *The Economics of Feasible Socialism Revisited.* London 1991 2nd edition [1969].

Pais, Abraham: *Niels Bohr's Times, In Physics, Philosophy and Polity.* Oxford 1991.

Parsons, Talcott: *The Structure of Social Action.* New York – London 1968 [1937, 1948].

Piketty, Thomas: *Capital in the Twenty-First Century.* Cambridge, Massachusetts 2014 [Paris 2013].

Popper, Karl Raimund: *The Open Society and Its Enemies.* London 1973 [1945, 1962, 1966].

Popper, Karl Raimund: *The Poverty of Historicism.* London 1986 [1957].

Poulantzas, Nicos: *Political Power and Social Classes.* London 1973 [Paris 1968].

Rigby, Stephen S.: *Marxism and History: A Critical Introduction.* 2nd edition Manchester 1998 [1st edition 1987].

Robinson, Joan: *An Essay on Marxian Economics.* London 1974, 2nd edition [1966; 1st edition 1942].

Sørensen, Curt: *Den europæiske deltagelseskrise – stormagtspolitik, massedeltagelse og ideologi i det 20. århundrede.* Frederiksberg 2017.

Sørensen, Curt: "Den historiske materialisme i lyset af nyere diskussion om social handlen og social objektivitet" *Politica* nr. 1, 23. årgang, 1991.

Sørensen, Curt: *Marxismen og den sociale orden.* Grenå 1976.

Therborn, Göran: "The Rule of Capital and the Rise of Democracy" *New Left Review* no 103, 1977.

Thing, Morten: *Hvad Marx og Engels mente med kommunisme? København* 2020.

Thompson, E. P.: *The Making of the English Working Class.* Harmondsworth, Middlesex 1968 [1963].

Thompson, E. P.: *The Poverty of Theory and Other Essays*. London 1978.

Timpanaro, Sebastiano: *On Materialism*. London 1975 [1970, 1973].

Wilkinson, Richard & Pickett, Kate: *The Spirit Level. Why Equality is Better for Everyone*. London 2010 [1st Edition London 2009].

Witt-Hansen, Johannes: *Historisk Materialisme*. København 1973.

Wright, Erik Olin: *Class, Crisis and the State*. London 1979 [1978].

Wright, Erik Olin: *Classes*. London 1985.

Wright, Erik Olin & Levine, Andrew & Sober, Elliott: *Reconstructing Marxism: Essays on Explanation and the Theory of History*. London 1992.